TEACHING

Outside

THE LINES

WITHDRAWN

*This one is for my grandchildren Paul, Miles, Theo, and London.
My hope is that this book helps your school become
a place that honors creativity.*

TEACHING *Outside* THE LINES

Developing *Creativity* in Every Learner

DOUG JOHNSON

CORWIN
A SAGE Company

FOR INFORMATION:

Corwin
A SAGE Company
2455 Teller Road
Thousand Oaks, California 91320
(800) 233-9936
www.corwin.com

SAGE Publications Ltd.
1 Oliver's Yard
55 City Road
London EC1Y 1SP
United Kingdom

SAGE Publications India Pvt. Ltd.
B 1/I 1 Mohan Cooperative Industrial Area
Mathura Road, New Delhi 110 044
India

SAGE Publications Asia-Pacific Pte. Ltd.
3 Church Street
#10-04 Samsung Hub
Singapore 049483

Executive Editor: Arnis Burvikovs
Associate Editor: Ariel Price
Editorial Assistant: Andrew Olson
Production Editor: Melanie Birdsall
Copy Editor: Diane DiMura
Typesetter: C&M Digitals (P) Ltd.
Proofreader: Alison Syring
Indexer: Amy Murphy
Cover and Interior Designer: Janet Kiesel
Marketing Manager: Lisa Lysne

Illustrations by Brady Johnson.

Printed in the United States of America

A catalog record of this book is available from the Library of Congress.

ISBN: 978-1-4833-7016-3

This book is printed on acid-free paper.

15 16 17 18 19 10 9 8 7 6 5 4 3 2 1

Contents

Acknowledgments

To Mary Mehsikomer and Anne Hanson—for reviewing the draft and adding great suggestions.

To Sir Ken Robinson who kicked all conscientious educators in the butt with his 2006 TED Talk on how schools are crushing creativity.

And as always, to the LWW for her continued support.

Publisher's Acknowledgments

Corwin gratefully acknowledges the contributions of the following reviewers:

Brad Gustafson
Principal
Plymouth, MN

Carol Holzberg
Technology Coordinator
Greenfield, MA

Alice Keeler
Educational Consultant
Fresno, CA

Kati Searcy
Teacher
Roswell, GA

Christopher Wells
Educational and Instructional Technology Consultant
Duluth, GA

About the Author

 **Doug Johnson** is the Director of Technology for the Burnsville-Eagan-Savage (MN) Public Schools and has served as an adjunct faculty member of Minnesota State University. His teaching experience has included work in Grades K–12 both here and in Saudi Arabia. He is the author of nine books, including *Learning Right From Wrong in the Digital Age*, *The Classroom Teacher's Technology Survival Guide*, and *Machines Are the Easy Part; People Are the Hard Part*. His columns appear in ASCD's *Educational Leadership* and in *Library Media Connection*. Doug's *Blue Skunk Blog* averages over 50,000 visits a month and his articles have appeared in over 40 books and periodicals. Doug has conducted workshops and given presentations for over 200 organizations throughout the United States and internationally and has held a variety of leadership positions in state and national organizations, including ISTE and AASL.

Introduction

How Did Vasco da Gama Spark My Interest in Creativity?

It's ironic that even as children are taught the accomplishments of the world's most innovative minds, their own creativity is being squelched.

—Jessica Olien (2013)

My fifth-grade grandson Paul was ready with his report on Vasco da Gama. He'd made a costume. He'd created props. He'd written a first-person autobiography to deliver. He was ready to dramatize a dull subject and make it fun for his classmates—and for himself.

Then his teacher announced that she did not allow props, costumes, or narrative reporting. Such devices would be "unfair to the rest of the class."

While this story originally angered me as both a grandparent and lifelong educator, it also spurred me into asking why Paul's teacher, an otherwise excellent educator as far as I could tell from other stories Paul told me of her classroom, chose to nip a creative approach to a history report in the bud. Why do some educators not only fail to encourage creativity in their students, but also seemingly discourage it?

The more I've studied the question, the more sympathetic I've become to educators and their often confusing and contradictory charges related to helping develop creativity in their students (see Figure 0.1).

Many of today's most successful people are creative. And creativity is growing in importance. Sir Ken Robinson has been excoriating educators (in a very charismatic way) for a rather long time about this. In his popular 2006 TED Talk, he observes, "creativity now is as important in education as literacy, and we should treat it with the same status" (Robinson, 2006).

Figure 0.1

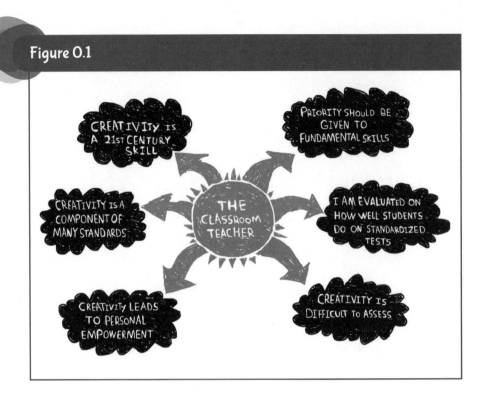

Do we in education simply pay a lot of lip service to encouraging creativity in kids, or do we actually believe all children can or should be creative individuals? We accept creativity in elective art classes. We throw in a "fun" writing assignment among the three-paragraph expository essays. We applaud when an athlete concocts and executes a clever play. But too often, we in education are compelled to discourage originality through stay-within-the-line rules, one-right-answer tests, must-be-followed templates, technology use that gives the illusion of creativity, and praise for conformity in thought and action in our discipline programs. We may feel compelled to do this because our society has decided to judge school and teacher effectiveness solely on the basis of test scores, but we are doing it nonetheless.

In hopes of changing our educational views of creativity, I've been studying, observing, conversing, and thinking about the relationship of education and people who color outside the lines. Many educators have been offering me insightful feedback to my blog posts, articles, and workshops on creativity in education. In other words, I've been learning all I can about creativity and then trying to figure out how educators can apply this knowledge in practical ways in all classrooms—how we can start teaching outside the lines as well.

I am far from the end of my journey of exploration into what makes people divergent thinkers, innovators, and creators—and how we as educators can help our students become more creative throughout their lives. But shall we travel together for a while, exploring some interesting questions?

Dangerous Delusions

Too many educators suffer from some common beliefs about creativity that are detrimental to children. Delusions are usually deep seated—and are not closely examined since they are held by such a large number of individuals. But let's get these myths out on the table anyway.

Delusion 1. Creative work does not belong in basic subjects like math, science, social studies, English, or "core" skill sets like information and technology literacy. Educators too often pigeon-hole creativity into arts classes—fine arts, fiction writing, music, theater, and dance. Of course creativity is an important part of these disciplines.

Yet we value creative problem solvers as much as we appreciate those folks who are creative in a more artistic sense. We need to extend the definition of *art* to dealing with people and situations in new and effective ways. The creativity many of us admire, especially in our coworkers and employees, is simply figuring out a way of accomplishing a task in a better way. Or dealing effectively with a problem—mechanical or human. We must never narrow what constitutes a "creative" endeavor.

Why do we restrict creativity to the art room and creative writing class when it should be in every subject, unit, and activity?

Delusion 2. Creativity does not require learning or discipline. When many of us look at an abstract painting, we may think something like, "Gee whiz, give (a) a monkey, (b) a little kid, or (c) me a can of paint and I can make a painting like that." We'd be wrong. Even abstract artists understand balance and tone and exhibit great craftsmanship and technical skills. The most original written ideas in the world are inaccessible when locked behind faulty grammar, spelling, syntax, or organization. Digital music composition programs like GarageBand do not cure a tin ear. Some of the most creative poetry follows the strict structures of the sonnet, villanelle, or haiku.

Too many students think that sufficient creativity will overcome a lack of skill or need for discipline or necessity for practice. Creativity unaccompanied by technical skills and knowledge (what this book will call *craftsmanship*), self-discipline, hard work, and practice isn't worth much.

Do we ask students to be both creative and disciplined? Should we set some parameters to creative activities?

Delusion 3. Creativity is just "icing on the cake" and we do not need to assess whether students can demonstrate it. "What gets measured, gets done" is a truism from the business world. If we ask students to demonstrate creativity or innovation, we need some tools to determine whether they have done so successfully. If we identify creativity as a true 21st century skill, is it fair to hold students to account for mastering it when we can't describe what it looks like, provide models, or be able to accurately determine whether it's been demonstrated?

How can we design and use assessments that address originality, effectiveness, and craftsmanship—the three key components of creativity?

Delusion 4. Only academically "gifted" children are creative. Sir Ken Robinson (2009) reminds educators that we should not be asking "if" a child is intelligent, but instead be asking "how" a child is intelligent. Let's riff on that statement by adding that we should not be asking "if" a child is creative, but "how" a child is creative.

Do we as educators need to honor multiple types of creativity, much as we now honor Gardner's multiple "intelligences?"

Delusion 5. Technology use automatically demands creativity. Anyone who has ever seen a slideshow with only large blocks of dry text and no graphic elements knows the fallacy of this assumption. A word-processed essay might be more legible, but not necessarily more novel, exciting, or moving. Many computer programs take no talent, thought, or originality to create products that look professional, giving the illusion of creativity. Even sophisticated 3-D printers, important players in the "maker" movement, are little more than expensive copy machines unless their use calls for originality.

What new opportunities does technology give students to demonstrate creativity? Do we run the risk of technology actually discouraging innovation and divergent thinking?

Delusion 6. Everyone wants creative students. Creative people have a long history of making others nervous or upset. From Elvis's gyrations, Monet's abstractions, Steve Jobs's technologies, to Gandhi's satyagraha—innovation is often met with resistance. Our students (and teachers) who are truly creative just might rattle our preconceptions and our sense of taste. Genuinely new products take some getting used to. Creativity often changes the nature of relationships, including the relationships between student and educator.

Do we recognize that creativity can upset the status quo and many educators, parents, and politicians want the status quo to stay, well, the status quo?

Delusion 7. Educators themselves do not need to display creativity. Students learn more from our examples than from our words. It's difficult to ask others to be creative when we don't exhibit creativity ourselves. If our own lessons are dull and uninspired, if our classrooms, libraries, and hallways are drab and lifeless, if we do not vocally support the creative efforts of other teachers, and if we don't try new approaches to teaching and learning, students will know us for the hypocrites we are.

Do we as educators need to be better risk takers, try new methods of instruction, even be subversive in order to help our students become more creative?

Albert Einstein is reported to have said, "Problems cannot be solved by the same level of thinking that created them." Given the state of our world, we desperately need higher levels of problem solving, ones that give creativity full reign. If we are going to help our kids color outside the lines, we will need to start teaching outside them as well.

A Note About Terms

Creativity	*Innovation*
Divergent thinking	*Invention*
Entrepreneurship	*Originality*
Imagination	*Out-of-the-box thinking*
Ingenuity	

I will be using these terms more-or-less interchangeably throughout this book.

Up for Discussion

1. Is it reasonable to hold classroom teachers accountable for developing creative thinking and problem solving in their students? Can creativity be taught?

2. On balance, which is more important: cultural literacy, basic skills, or creativity?

3. What common misperceptions do you see among educators related to creativity?

The Rise of the Creative Class(room)

Why Is Creativity No Longer a "Nice Extra" in Education?

In order to navigate the New Realities you have to be creative—not just within your particular profession, but in everything... this is true for everybody. Janitors, receptionists, and bus drivers, too. The game has just been ratcheted up a notch.

—Hugh MacLeod (2009)

Why Does Apple Have So Much Money?

How does that $600 you just spent on your last Apple iPhone get distributed among those who participated in its production? According to one study (Kraemer, Linden, & Dedrick, 2011), only about 40 percent of what you paid for the device was for materials, labor, and shipping. Apple and its shareholders got the rest—as profits.

Primarily for being creative.

Creativity = making money.

Creativity is a vocational skill.

Creativity may be the only way people can stay employed in good jobs in a postindustrial, automated, global economy. Like it or not.

Gone Missing

There are a number of workers I just don't see much of anymore . . .

- I don't see human attendants when entering or leaving parking lots.

- I don't talk to check-in people at the airline counters anymore. My credit card talks to the machine that prints out my boarding pass.

- I am seeing fewer bank tellers and supermarket clerks.

- My children think I am telling tall tales when I tell them that I once had "people" who pumped my gas, washed my car windows, filled my tires, and sometimes even gave me a free drinking glass as a gift when I went to a gas station.

- I don't hear the voice of a human telephone operator, tech support, or reservation clerks until I've waded through a half dozen phone menus who politely, but often maddeningly, give me the information I'm seeking.

- I don't know many people who work in manufacturing now who don't program the robots that do the repetitive tasks more precisely than humans ever did.

It's not like we've not seen this coming. Way back in 2004, professors Frank Levy and Richard Murnane (2004) studied the kind of jobs that had already been increasing and decreasing in the years between 1969 and 1999. They found that jobs requiring "complex communications" grew by nearly 15 percent and jobs requiring "expert thinking" grew by about 6 percent, while jobs requiring "routine cognitive work" and "routine manual work" declined. This study was updated in 2013—and the findings are still accurate (Autor & Price, 2013).

The people whose places have been taken by automatic tellers, self-service equipment, robotics, and menu-driven telephone help trees fall into the "routine" categories. The information given and processes performed are standardized—multiple-choice answers, if you will. For any situation that arises that calls for something more than an A, B, C, or D response, a supervisor must be found—one who can think "expertly" and be a creative problem solver.

In today's economy, machines or workers in developing nations do simple things less expensively—and often more precisely. And do we really want our students aspiring to mindless, repetitive work?

Right Brain Skills, the Creative Class, and Luddites

In his book *A Whole New Mind: Why Right-Brainers Will Rule the Future*, Daniel Pink (2006) asks the reader if his job can be done better by a machine or less expensively in another country. But the most interesting question he asks is this: "Am I offering something that satisfies the nonmaterial, transcendent desires of an abundant age?" (p. 232).

In other words, Pink predicts that when one has the money and is given a choice, a consumer will purchase a product that not only works, but has something value added. An aesthetic appeal, for example. It will be these creative folks, those who use the right sides of their brains, who are less likely to lose their jobs to factory workers in China or to a robot.

Richard Florida (2003) writes about the group he calls the "Creative Class." He estimates that about 30 percent of the US workforce can be categorized as creatives, divided between the Super Creative Core and Creative Professionals. (Remember these distinctions when we examine Big-C and little-c definitions of creativity in Chapter 4.) These people and their companies earn enough money that cities attempt to lure them as residents—as opposed to trying to have their jobs outsourced to Bangladesh.

The outsourcing and automating trend is now impacting a new set of workers: those in traditional white-collar jobs. *New York Times* economics columnist Paul Krugman (2012) thinks Luddites, the 18th-century English textile workers who were threatened by automation, got a bad rap. He writes that "the workers hurt most were those who had, with effort, acquired valuable skills—only to find those skills suddenly devalued." Today's "Luddites" are x-ray technicians, legal researchers, computer programmers, and other skilled occupations. A college degree alone no longer offers a lock on full-time, lifelong employment at a good salary.

Business gets this. In response to this rapidly and dramatically changing economic landscape, the 2010 IBM poll of 1,500 CEOs identified creativity as the number one "leadership competency" of the future (IBM, 2010).

We as conscientious educators cannot ignore these employment trends.

What Do Our Educational Standards Say?

Obviously I am not the only, and certainly not the first, educator who has figured out that schools need to start thinking about creativity as an important skill students must develop.

In 2000, Benjamin Bloom's famous taxonomy of learning objectives was revised by some of his previous students (Anderson & Krathwohl, 2001). *Creating*, with its sub-descriptors of designing, constructing, planning, producing, inventing, devising, and making, became the highest of the higher-order thinking skills.

The International Society for Technology in Education (ISTE; 2007) in its widely used National Educational Technology Standards require students to "demonstrate creative thinking, construct knowledge, and develop innovative products and processes using technology."

The American Association of School Librarians's (2007) standards demand students "demonstrate creativity by using multiple resources and formats" and "use creative and artistic formats to express personal learning."

The International Baccalaureate program (2014) core requirements include CAS—creativity, action, and service—stating "creativity provides students with the opportunity to explore their own sense of original thinking and expression."

In their Framework Definitions document, the Partnership for 21st Century Skills (2011) lists "Think Creatively," "Work Creatively with Others," and "Implement Innovations" as key student outcomes.

Look carefully at thoughtful, forward thinking, recognized standards in your region or organization. Do they recognize creativity as a valuable skill students will need to be successful in education, in their careers, and in life?

Creativity and Engagement

In the workshops on "Net Generation learners" that I give, I ask participants to describe some ways today's kids' lives, values, and experiences are different from when we were children. One common response is that "today's kids need to be constantly entertained."

I would challenge that observation because too many of us confuse the terms *entertainment* and *engagement*. Here is how I differentiate the terms:

- Entertainment's primary purpose is to provide an enjoyable experience; engagement's primary purpose is to focus attention so learning occurs.

- Entertainment is ephemeral, often frivolous; engagement creates long-lasting results and deals with important skills and subjects.

- Entertainment needs have little relevance to the reader/watcher/listener; engaging experiences most often relate directly to the learner.

- Entertainment is an escape from problems; engagement involves solving problems.

- Entertain is often passive; engagement is active or interactive.

and especially

- Entertainment is the result of the creativity of others; engagement asks for creativity on the part of the learner (see Figure 1.1).

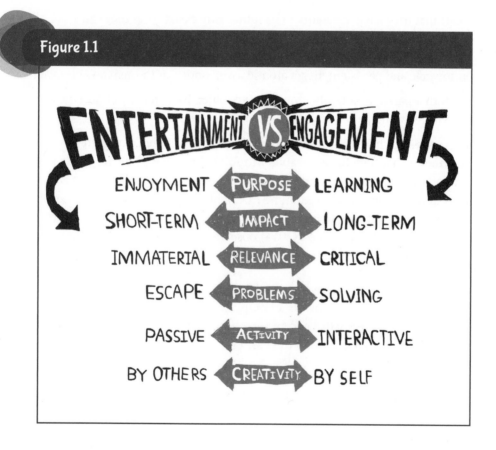

Figure 1.1

As an increasing number of students carry in their pockets or backpacks devices that can both entertain *and* engage, teachers need to know and remember the difference between the terms. Allowing or asking students to create—and not simply consume—turn these devices into tools for education. True, kids may still be distracted from our lectures and worksheets, but when in the act of creation, they will at least be productively distracted. We'll visit this topic again in Chapter 7.

Completing an education that allows entry into both the workplace and society is critical for every student today. When our society truly can no longer afford to leave any child behind, it will be engagement by encouraging creativity in learning that may help us reach every child.

The Most Important Reason Kids Need to Learn to Be Creative

So far, we've looked at creativity as a vocational skill, a work skill, a means to secure good jobs.

But idealist that I am, I also want students who feel empowered, knowing at heart that they have the ability to be sufficiently clever. That they can solve any problem they encounter. That they don't have to simply take what life throws at them and live with it. That there is always a way, if one is sufficiently innovative and persistent, to get around, over, under, or through any obstacle.

As both a parent and teacher, my primary objective is for my children to be able to get along just fine without me.

Far too many children leave school without the confidence or even realization that they have the ability to solve their own problems. They rely on parents, teachers, or perceived leaders to present "the solution" to issues that trouble them. As we'll examine in Chapter 10, schools have had the historic societal charge to create conformists, order takers, and in-the-box thinkers. But as David Brooks (2014) observes about that student who has a perfect academic record applying for a job,

> this person has followed the cookie-cutter formula for what it means to be successful and you [as an employer] actually have no clue what the person is really like except for a high talent for social conformity. Either they have no desire to chart out an original life course or lack the courage to do so. Shy away from such people.

As a lifelong educator, my mantra has always been that my mission is to create thinkers, not believers. A large part of thinking should be thinking creatively as a means of solving our own problems, solving the problems of society, and understanding that we all have the power to choose the paths we take in life.

I love the everyday MacGyver-like innovators I encounter—both children and adults. I respect those individuals who see an obstacle as something akin to a jungle gym—a chance to not just climb but to get joy and satisfaction in doing so. I admire people who see their lives not as something into which they were born, but something they've created.

Can you think of a better reason that students need to practice creativity?

How Are Schools Doing in Creating Creative Students?

Sadly, studies show that schools in the United States have not succeeded in helping foster creativity but are doing just the opposite. We're crushing the creativity right out of kids. According to one study, creativity scores had been going up, paralleling IQ scores until about 1990. Then boom—down they went. Says the study's author Kyung Hee Kim, "It's very clear, and the decrease is very significant." It is the scores of younger children in America—from kindergarten through sixth grade—for whom the decline is "most serious" (Bronson & Merryman, 2010). She observes further (Townsend, 2014) that

> children have become less emotionally expressive, less energetic, less talkative and verbally expressive, less humorous, less imaginative, less unconventional, less lively and passionate, less perceptive, less apt to connect seemingly irrelevant things, less synthesizing, and less likely to see things from a different angle.

Our educational system does a good job of rewarding social conformity and building a one-right-answer mentality. In his book *Savage Inequalities*, Jonathan Kozol (1992), after examining schools in East St. Louis, Chicago, New York City, Camden, Cincinnati, and Washington, DC, concludes that two separate public school systems operate in the United States:

> Children in one set of schools are educated to be governors; children in the other set of schools are trained for being governed. The former are given the imaginative range to mobilize ideas for economic growth; the latter are provided with the discipline to do the narrow tasks the first group will prescribe. (p. 176)

The obvious culprit, of course, is our American obsession with testing. Drilling students ad nauseum—that there is always one right answer. While it is a noble goal to make sure all students, regardless of social class or ability, can demonstrate the basics of reading, writing, and mathematics and have core knowledge about science and the social sciences, this bar is set too low and two narrowly. Basic skills without the confidence to apply them in new situations will still leave children behind.

Testing, however, is a topic for another book. Instead of looking for excuses, let's look for some solutions.

Up for Discussion

1. Do educators need to reexamine their perceptions of what skills students need to be successful in today's economy? How are today's skills and dispositions different from those needed by previous generations?

2. Can judging whether graduates are "career and college ready," the worthy goal of many K–12 schools, be done solely on the basis of standardized test scores? Do teachers need to assess more than the basics?

3. Does the attention given to creativity in a school system separate graduates into the categories of "the governors" or "the governed"? Can it be argued that developing self-sufficient, empowered individuals who have both the skills and confidence to solve their own problems is the hallmark of an effective school?

I Can't Define It, But I Know It When I See It

What Is Creativity Anyway?

Learn the rules like a pro, so you can break them like an artist.

—Pablo Picasso

Ms. Najran asked her class to create campaign posters that creatively addressed the problem of trash in the high school hallways. It was a good assignment that nearly everyone in the school felt made an impact on the litter problem.

But when it came time to give a grade for the posters, Ms. Najran got some pushback from her students. "How can you say one project was more creative than another?" "A mashup is a creative work!" "Mike's poster was a complete rip-off of another advertisement." "That poster has a great concept, but the drawings are terrible and it has a misspelling on it."

Given the controversy over the project, Ms. Najran wound up asking students to vote on which posters they deemed to be most effective—not most "creative." This proved to be more acceptable to the students.

When you or I use the term *creativity* what exactly are we talking about? Before I started purposely examining this subject, my attitude toward creativity was that while I couldn't define it, I knew it when I saw it.

In education, something that cannot be defined cannot be assessed. At least objectively. And if you can't measure an ability, many educators ask if it has value, especially in our current political climate of accountability in which performance data is so important.

The 100+ Definitions of Creativity

I am not the only one who struggles with the definition of creativity. There are over 100 definitions of creativity as it relates to education in the research literature (Treffinger, Young, Selby, Shepardson, & Center for Creative Learning, 2002).

While I can't claim to have read them all, those definitions that I have examined nearly always have two components in common. First, that creativity has an element of the new, the innovative, the original— something not yet done before or done in a new way. This is not surprising.

But the second, too often overlooked, shared element in most definitions is that creativity adds value to the task or objective to which it is applied. Not only must the approach be new, it must make the product, the procedure, the message, or the experience more effective. To me, that second piece gives educators one key to valid creativity assessment.

We must be asking not just if the work is original, but how that originality improves the end result. Creativity guru Sir Ken Robinson (2006) simply says creativity is "the process of having original ideas that have value."

Craftsmanship—The Missing Element

But perhaps even Sir Ken's definition is missing an important element. Creativity that has value depends on what I'll call *craftsmanship* as well (see Figure 2.1).

What is craftsmanship? In a sense, it is the ability to shape new ideas while still conforming to reality. It's the "why" any new idea has value. It's what makes the idea feasible. It's why we spend all that time doing all the other skill building and knowledge acquisition in education. And it's why, when craftsmanship is used a part of the definition of creativity, new ideas outnumber genuine solutions many times over.

Marc Tucker (2014), president of the National Center on Education and the Economy, argues that international comparisons of educational

Figure 2.1

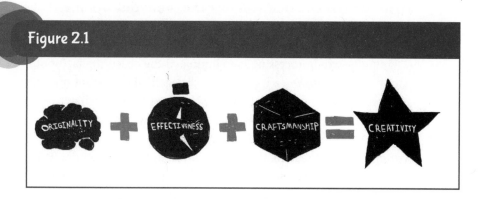

systems based on test scores such as PISA (The Program for International Student Assessment) do have value, even in economies that need creative workers. He writes:

> *Creativity does not take place in a knowledge vacuum. It is typically the product of the rubbing together, so to speak, of two or more bodies of knowledge, of holding up the framework associated with one body of knowledge to another arena that it was not designed to illuminate.*

Craftsmanship is what separates cacophony from music or scribbles from art or fantasies from genuine solutions to a problem.

So what is craftsmanship? I'm calling each of these factors a type of "craft":

1. **Content knowledge that makes an original idea workable.** Knowing the properties of baking soda in a new recipe is necessary if the cook hopes to bake an edible dish. Understanding current accounting principles—income versus expense, for example—is needed by the most innovative entrepreneur. Before my dentist tries a new procedure in fixing my root canal, I'm praying as that drill comes closer that he's paid attention in dental school and knows human anatomy—especially where nerves are located. When Whip Whitaker in the movie *Flight* flipped his plane upside down in order to keep it from crashing and burning, he was able to do so since he understood aerodynamic properties of flight and airplane design.

   Much debate has centered about the need for all students being culturally literate—a core set of knowledge and skills as described by E.D. Hirsh and others. One relatively simple question of those who ask students to learn large amounts of basic information is "Why memorize something that is easy to look up?" If creativity cannot take place in a "knowledge vacuum," some foundation knowledge which provides context to problems is not just necessary, but critical.

2. **Written literacies that enhance the communication.** As I once cautioned my suffering composition students, even the best ideas can be hidden behind poor spelling, punctuation, or sentence structure. (Thankfully, word processing has eliminated the obscuring factor of poor handwriting.) Yes, e e cummings disregarded capitalization rules and Daniel Webster, George Bernard Shaw, and other notables invented their own spelling systems. But when writing a persuasive essay or a short story, most of us do well to conform to standard writing practice, breaking the rules by intention, not ignorance. For one's ideas to be taken seriously in many situations, one's language needs to conform to professional and cultural standards.

3. **Design skills that add clarity and aesthetic value.** We've all seen multimedia presentations that are not just dull, but maybe difficult to comprehend because of poor color choices, hard-to-read fonts, or irrelevant graphics. As transliteracy, the ability to communicate in multiple formats including video, photography, and, graphics, becomes increasingly essential in more fields, poor visual design becomes the illiteracy of the YouTube age. Given the degree to which our society has moved toward communicating visually and auditorily (YouTube is the world's second largest search engine), transilliteracy is perhaps an even greater handicap than verbal illiteracy.

4. **Discipline (physical dexterity developed through practice) that allows a performer to be expressive.** The proper bowing of a violinist that allows a new interpretation of an old song comes from hours of practice. Great athletes hone their abilities through practice and exercise. Artists may sketch countless forms before starting a work. Writers write experimental work only for themselves. Practice often separates genius from mediocrity.

5. **Accepting the illogical nature of human beings in interpersonal relationships when leading or managing a group.** If we were all Vulcans who are ruled by logic, unburdened by emotion, it would probably be a whole lot easier to be a leader—and far more boring. Knowing that praise works as a motivator, that perception is reality for many people, that empathy is a requirement in making good decisions—simple, or perhaps not so simple— understanding of human nature is another form of craftsmanship. Original solutions to problems that offend, frighten, or confuse those to whom they are suggested or not "sold" in an effective manner are as doomed as those that cannot work for physical reasons.

6. **Working within limits: of resources, of time, of morality, and of social acceptability.** There are many simple solutions to complex problems that are simply unworkable. (Really, can't we just ship all of

our most trouble-making students to a different school, state, country, or universe? Can't we just deal with that climate change thing by simply outlawing all personally owned vehicles?) Creative people understand that solutions to problems have to fit real-word conditions—both personal and social. Most political arguments are the result of different people having different understandings of those limits.

7. **Working within the constraints of an assignment.** Do we as teachers stifle creativity when we require having three supporting arguments in a paper, ten sources of information in a project, a limit of seven minutes for a presentation, a project that uses the scientific method, or a poem that follows the rules of the haiku? Good craftsmanship recognizes restraints that may be externally imposed on a product. Those exhibiting mastery of a form of craftsmanship don't just follow those requirements, but use them as a launch pad to more innovative thinking. Placing conditions and constraints on an assignment may actually increase the innovation shown by students.

We call the natural ability some people have at these crafts *talent* or *giftedness*.

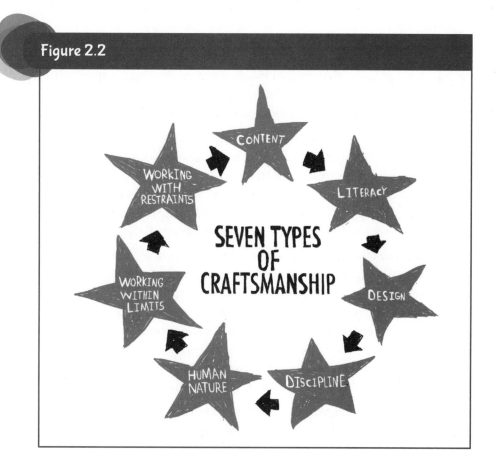

Figure 2.2

SEVEN TYPES OF CRAFTSMANSHIP

CONTENT

LITERACY

DESIGN

DISCIPLINE

HUMAN NATURE

WORKING WITHIN LIMITS

WORKING WITH RESTRAINTS

This is why we still need educational standards—whether they are the Common Core (or the next magic bullet), discipline-specific standards, professional standards, common rules of writing and mathematics, or the ability to read. These help give students the foundations that build craftsmanship.

It's been argued that the creative process is actually enhanced when the demands of craftsmanship get stronger. The more seemingly impossible the task, the greater the need for original thinking. Think of why escape movies are so entertaining—the more secure the prison, the more remote the island, the larger the guard—the greater the need for innovation. The more one knows about a field, the more likely she is to make a meaningful contribution. (To be fair, a case for naïveté can also be made—becoming too entrenched in the "rules" can make one myopic as well.)

Creative ideas are like diamonds—the greater the pressure during creation, the greater the value. Asking students to be creative does not mean throwing out rules, skills, or knowledge. It simply means using those important competencies in new and useful ways. Asking teachers to develop creativity does not mean throwing out standards. It simply means taking those important standards and expanding them in important ways.

Measuring Creativity as an Innate Talent

Social scientists have attempted to measure native intelligence quotient (IQ) since the late 19th century through testing. And similar testing has been done to measure innate creative abilities, but this work is more recent.

During World War II, the air force asked J. P. Guilford, a psychologist at the University of Southern California, to create a measuring tool that would help determine which pilots, when confronted with a mechanical failure, would act with an "original behavior" that would prevent disaster. Such behavior wasn't measured by IQ testing. Guilford's work became the tests for divergent thinking (Csikszentmihalyi, 1997).

If you are interested in some attempts at the "objective" measurements of creative abilities, the Center for Creative Learning website has two databases with information about 100 tools for assessing creativity including checklists and tests. These are worth investigating if you would like to see how academic scholars approach creativity or want some pre- or post-metrics for a research project that studies building the creative capacity of kids. And I would highly recommend Treffinger et al.'s (2002) authoritative guide, *Assessing Creativity: A Guide for Educators*.

Personally, I want attention to creativity to be part of every child's daily work. And I hold the belief that formative assessments can provide the tools we need to accomplish this task. We'll look at this in more depth in Chapters 3 and 8.

Fanning the Spark of Creativity

All humans have an imagination—it's what separates us to a large extent from other animals. All human beings have the capacity for innovation. Human beings are inherently problem solvers.

So you might rightly ask, "Why do we all not display creativity? Why do so many adults and children seem to fatalistically take life as it comes rather than take circumstances into their own hands through creative thought and action?"

It's because creativity, no matter how fierce, no matter how important, no matter how original, isn't worth anything unless it is accompanied by some corollary skills that give it life. Creativity is often described as a spark. And as we know, sparks quickly burn out unless fanned into flames. It's this fanning work that creates a useful fire as every good Boy and Girl Scout knows.

Treffinger and his cohorts in his comprehensive guide (mentioned above) establish four "personal creativity characteristics": Generating Ideas, Digging Deeper Into Ideas, Openness and Courage to Explore Ideas, and Listening to One's "Inner Voice." The first two relate closely to divergent and convergent thinking—important but standard items included in most definitions of creativity.

But it is the third and fourth characteristics that we too often overlook in helping students develop their innovative potential. Treffinger et al. (2002) define them as

> The openness and courage to explore ideas category includes some personality traits that relate to one's interests, experiences, attitudes, and self-confidence. The characteristics in this category . . . include problem sensitivity, aesthetic sensitivity, curiosity, sense of humor, playfulness, fantasy and imagination, risk-taking, tolerance for ambiguity, tenacity, openness to experience, emotional sensitivity, adaptability, intuition, willingness to grow, unwillingness to accept authoritarian assertions without critical examination, and integration of dichotomies or opposites. (p. 15)

> The listening to one's "inner voice" category includes traits that involve a personal understanding of who you are, a vision of where you want to go, and a commitment to do whatever it takes to get there. The characteristics in this category . . . include awareness of

creativeness, persistence or perseverance, self-direction, internal locus of control, introspective, freedom from stereotyping, concentration, energy, and work ethic. (p. 16)

I would define these as dispositions or mindsets. And without them, the most wonderful creative spark will die out. Treffinger et al.'s description is wonderful, but let's condense this into a bit more manageable list.

Grit

Thanks to the TED Talk by Angela Lee Duckworth (2013), *grit*—or what might be called tenacity or perseverance—is becoming a popular educational term. Grit scores, studies show, are more highly correlated to success than IQ. Getting kids to stick with a task, project, or practice is a vital component of creativity. Creative ideas don't always work the first time.

Empathy

Understanding the needs and viewpoints of others is a critical ability for many types of creativity. Authors understand the needs of their readers. Designers sense what has appeal. Good salespeople know what their customers want. And I believe there are ways to increase our capacity for empathy. Reading fiction and biographies about people who are in circumstances much different from our own is among the most powerful ways to develop a capacity for empathy (Johnson, 2009).

Courage and Risk Tolerance

Creativity means doing things in new ways and understanding that the new is not always understood or appreciated, and may even be widely criticized, especially when introduced. Having the will to continue in the face of disapproval takes courage and tolerance for risk. And remember that children, as they grow, spend a lot of time, energy, and worry conforming to peer norms.

Growth Mindset

Carol Dweck (2006) argues that people who are happiest and most successful believe that they and others are not simply born with a set of abilities, but have the capacity to grow, learn, and become more intelligent. She argues that the number one ingredient in creative achievement is the resilience created by a growth mindset.

Self-Esteem and Confidence

People with good opinions of themselves, who value their own ideas, who have confidence in their judgement are more likely to experiment.

Much of this is gained by having success in the past, having good mentors and parents, and knowing just how much to bite off in any given enterprise.

Curiosity

Natural or teacher-inspired curiosity about a topic or problem leads to exploration with creative theories, experiments, and solutions being an outgrowth of curiosity. This is why the personalization movement in education—allowing students' own interests to drive their learning—is effective not just for teaching content knowledge and skill acquisition, but for developing innovative thinkers as well.

Independence and Subversiveness

Let's face it, people try a new thing simply because they are not happy with the old thing. And many establishments and the people in them are pretty determined to keep things just the way they are. For both students and teachers, entrenched in a model of 20th century schooling, impatience with change engenders subversiveness—the active, but often disguised, actions deliberately designed to undermine "education as we know it" (or business as we know it, or science as we know it, or art as we know it, etc.).

Another of Einstein's Internet-gleaned quotes says, "Make everything as simple as possible, but not simpler." I would suggest that while defining and describing creativity and the dispositions needed to make it valuable we don't ignore the complexity or the mystery of the process, but that neither do we let those factors keep us from recognizing and teaching creativity in our work with students—and each other.

It's critical that when asking for creativity, we are not tossing out standards, skills, or content knowledge. It's imperative we recognize that creativity without the dispositions, especially grit, that turn the creative idea into a product with value.

Up for Discussion

1. How important is having a working definition of *creativity*? Can we as educators rely on simply knowing it when we see it?

2. How should education balance teaching basic skills, cultural and content area knowledge, and creativity? Which should be given priority?

3. Is there value in measuring creativity through testing as an innate ability much as we measure intelligence through IQ testing? If so, how should the results of such testing be used?

4. If tolerance for risk taking is a critical disposition of creative individuals, how can teachers build that tolerance in students?

The One-Right-Answer Testing Mentality

Why Are Schools Failing to Produce Creative Graduates?

It is quite strange how little effect school—even high school—seems to have had on the lives of creative people. Often one senses that, if anything, school threatened to extinguish the interest and curiosity that the child had discovered outside its walls.

—Mihaly Csikszentmihalyi (1997)

As a former librarian, I have never lost my desire to read aloud to an audience. While I have finally stopped using hand puppets (at least with adult groups), I still sneak a picture book into my workshops now and again. And one of my favorites in Miriam Cohen's picture book *First Grade Takes a Test.*

The book describes the frustrations and problems that arise when Danny's class is given a test to determine who might qualify for a gifted and talented program. During the normed, multiple choice, paper-and-pencil test, he and his classmates find it difficult to answer questions like "What do rabbits eat?" "What do firemen do?" and "Which person in a drawing is taller?"

Some students, based on their personal experiences, are stumped by the fact that their own "right" answers do not appear as choices. Even though one student thoughtfully draws in a "correct" answer to a question, the test selects a single student, Anna Maria, to be included in the pull-out program.

Ironically, the remaining children creatively resolve an argument over who received a larger cookie by weighing rather than measuring the cookies. And the teacher reminds the class:

> The test doesn't tell all the things you can do! You can build things! You can read books! You can make pictures! You have good ideas! And another thing. The test doesn't tell you if you are a kind person who helps your friend. Those are important things.

If there is a simpler or more elegant criticism of standardized testing, I haven't found it. Schooling in the United States would be a happier and more effective place were all politicians and employees of the Department of Education required to read Cohen's little book. And discuss it. Maybe create a poster. Or sing a song about it.

Combatting the One-Right-Answer Mentality

Using testing as a sole or primary means of assessing student ability has strangled the development of creativity in too many of our children. As we discussed in Chapter 2, craftsmanship (content knowledge and skills) is a critical component of innovative ideas that have value. No doubt about it. But how do we balance this need for factual knowledge and basic skills with the demands of promoting divergent thinking? Without perverting the use of objective testing as our family likes to do, as shown in Figure 3.1.

First we need to acknowledge as educators that formative assessments are better learning tools than many summative assessments, especially standardized tests.

Extrinsic Motivation and a Fear of Taking Risks

In his book *Punished by Rewards,* Alfie Kohn (1999) outlines the deleterious impact that extrinsic motivation—including test scores—has on learning.

Figure 3.1

> **WHAT FALLS FROM THE SKY AND TURNS THE GROUND WHITE?**
>
> ☐ SNOW
> ☐ RAIN
> ☐ DUST
> ☐ OTHER
>
> *GIVE AN ANSWER NOT ON THE LIST.*

Through examples and research, he demonstrates five reasons rewards fail: Rewards can punish those who do not receive them; rewards can rupture relationships between students and between students and teachers; rewards ignore the reasons for a desired behavior; rewards can discourage risk taking; and rewards can actually discourage desired behaviors.

Didn't the research in Chapter 2 show that *risk taking* is one of the hallmarks of a creative person?

Poor first-grader George in Cohen's book, when confronted with the question of what rabbits eat on the standardized test, carefully drew a carrot on the test form since he knew from personal experience that a rabbit's teeth needed to be constantly worn down by eating such foods. Not only did George get no credit for his original and correct response, but he may believe the next time that such thinking not only earns him no reward (a good test grade) but punishes him for challenging the authority of the test itself.

Such aversion to risk taking is common among all students, but especially among those that take pride in their scholastic accomplishments—those A students who have high academic goals and feel they need the straight A's and high SAT scores to get into their choice of college (and remain members of good standing in a family who places high value on such measurements).

I would also argue that dependence on test scores discourages innovative teaching as well. Teaching to the test, teaching good test-taking strategies, and ignoring any skills or subjects not tested, are all adaptations even conscientious, caring teachers are making as test scores are the sole measurements of both personal and school effectiveness. Talk about discouraging risk taking! And in an educational system that is failing too many of students, risk taking may be the only ethical professional behavior.

Technology consultant Jim Moulton (2009) observes:

> Let's say we bring a group of kids into the art room and tell them they can do whatever they want. Will they become creative? I always thought the answer to this was yes, but turns out the answer is no.

> What the vast majority will tend to do is replicate earlier efforts for which they have been praised—those efforts they have perceived as successful. In other words, people will do over what they have already done.

How likely is a child to write creatively when he knows his teacher gives top grades for formal writing? How likely is a student to suggest an innovative approach to a research problem when the number of sources count more than questioning those sources? Will a high school student take an elective art class knowing that she is sure to ace an academic class that requires little more than regurgitating textbook and lecture notes on the final but may get a lower grade in other electives that may take a more subjective approach to assessment?

This is not a small problem. This is a deep deficiency in how we determine student learning and abilities.

Formative and Authentic Assessments as Creativity Builders

At the risk of grossly oversimplifying the wonderful work by Benjamin Bloom, Robert Marzano, Paul Black, Dylan Wiliam, and other scholars, I would simply say that summative assessments, especially standardized tests, are about ranking students (and their schools, teachers, principals, superintendents, school boards, and departments of education).

Formative assessments are tools that help students grow.

Formative assessments provide feedback in real time so that the teacher can, as best teaching practices suggest, "monitor and adjust" his or her instruction. They let the teacher know in which areas a student is proficient and where that student needs more help or practice. Unlike a summative assessment, no student is labeled a permanent C+ student or not performing at grade level. Intrinsic rather than extrinsic motivation increases. Formative assessment increases students' self-knowledge and sense of personal responsibility for their own learning. Formative assessment provides the teacher with the information to differentiate learning for every student—to consider varied approaches for students with different learning styles to ensure everyone has a chance at success. The focus and philosophy is on growth with the understanding that time needed to master a skill is the variable, not a student's genetic ability (Dodge, 2009).

David Nicol and Debra Macfarlane-Dick (2006) summarize seven principles of good feedback. Effective feedback

1. Clarifies what good performance is (goals, criteria, expected standards),

2. Facilitates the development of self-assessment in learning,

3. Provides high-quality information to students about their learning,

4. Encourages teacher and peer dialogue around learning,

5. Encourages positive motivational beliefs and self-esteem,

6. Provides opportunities to close the gap between current and desired performance, and

7. Provides information to teachers that can be used to help shape teaching.

It is, in essence, an informed dialogue between the teacher and the student about what that student knows and can do. One effective type of formative assessment is conversation among students related to their learning as well— building relationships as opposed to destroying them as Kohn warns the competition inherent in extrinsic motivation—scores on tests—tends to do. Peer review, peer assessment, and peer construction of quality criteria give students practice in whole-life skills.

Authentic assessment—assessments that rely on performance, application of skills and knowledge, and collections of student work (portfolios)—when used as intended, is a powerful form of formative assessment. Performance assessment means passing the driving part of the driving test not just the written test. And aren't you glad people aren't allowed to drive until they can demonstrate they can steer, brake, and stay on the correct side of the road?

Formative assessments can be done in a variety of ways. Judith Dodge (2009), in her short, readable, and informative guide, *25 Quick Formative Assessments for a Differentiated Classroom,* categorizes four different types of formative assessments.

- **Summaries and reflections.** Students stop and reflect, make sense of what they have heard or read, derive personal meaning from their learning experiences, and/or increase their metacognitive skills. These require that students use content-specific language.

- **Lists, charts, and graphic organizers.** Students will organize information, make connections, and note relationships through the use of various graphic organizers.

- **Visual representations of information.** Students will use both words and pictures to make connections and increase memory, facilitating retrieval of information later on. This "dual coding" helps teachers address classroom diversity, preferences in learning style, and different ways of "knowing."

- **Collaborative activities.** Students have the opportunity to move and/or communicate with others as they develop and demonstrate their understanding of concepts.

Thankfully, Dodge includes step-by-step instructions on specific activities that help teachers conduct these assessments.

Technology and Formative Assessment

One of the most exciting ways technology is being used in today's classroom is as a communications tool. Remember that formative assessment is about establishing dialogue. Here are a few specific ways technology strengthens communication leading to more powerful formative assessments:

1. **Student response systems.** Whether dedicated devices like Senteos used with interactive whiteboards or personally owned student devices (laptops, tablets, smartphones, netbooks) using response systems applications with Web-based feedback tools, immediate results can be shown to the entire class or just viewed by the instructor. Among the more popular free tools now available are Socrative, PollEverywhere, GoogleForms, and GoSoapBox.

2. **Cloud-based tools used for collaboration and feedback.** GoogleApps for Education, Microsoft 365, and Zoho, among other products, are an effective means of sharing work and providing comments. The ability to share at a variety of levels—view, comment, edit, or chat—make this a must-have resource for both feedback from teachers, parents, and fellow students.

3. **Brainstorming tools.** Tired of those sticky notes falling off your whiteboard? Nifty tools like Padlet, Mindmeister, and TodaysMeet allow online sharing of plans and ideas in real time. Whole-group viewing reduces redundancy in ideas—and often one idea sparks others.

4. **Web-based creation tools.** Animoto, Prezi, Wordle, VoiceThread, and a multitude of infographic creators like Creately make professional-looking graphics and presentations relatively simple. A word of warning—in Chapter 7, we'll discuss that just because something looks nice, doesn't make it creative.

5. **Cameras and microphones used to record performances.** Many schools choose tablet computers rather than laptops for a simple reason—their built-in cameras and microphones let children communicate with photos, video, and audio. When kids record their own actions, these devices become formative assessment tools of the highest order. Watching myself give a talk once when I played with the change in my pocket improved my public-speaking skill. Now I always present with empty pockets. Recorded work can also be shared with a broad audience, including parents, peers, and the community, leading to a higher level of concern about the quality of one's work.

6. **Differentiation of instruction by providing digital learning materials that fit a variety of learning styles and reading abilities.** Used in conjunction with content/course management system like Moodle, e-books, full-text data-based, and Open Educational Resources like Khan Academy, rich materials and lessons are provided for any ability level of students, both at school and at home. When the formative assessment shows some students need extra help, we need to be able to provide that help with a different reading level of material or a better way to watch a video.

7. **Using online storage areas to curate, collect, and share student work that becomes a portfolio.** Our district uses GoogleSites to help students in Grades 6–12 store and organize their work each year. A record of work completed can be powerful evidence of one's suitability for a job or an advanced educational program.

Let's go back to George with whom this chapter started. Had he the opportunity to explain to his teacher why he drew that carrot on his test page, his teacher would know that he understood the question, that he knows the properties of rabbits and their eating habits, and that he had the personal courage to offer a better, more accurate answer to the question. George would have felt supported in his divergent thinking rather than being penalized by it.

And he may be motivated to challenge authority in the future through a creative act or product.

Up for Discussion

1. Have educational reformers focused too much on summative assessments, most norm referenced? What is being measured by state, national, and international tests?

2. How can one design a summative assessment that allows for creativity?

3. Does the "one-right-answer" mentality work for today's economy and workforce? If so, when?

4. On the job, do workers encounter formative or summative assessments? Which is most likely to lead to creative solutions to challenges in the workplace?

The ~~Dog~~ Chupacabra Ate My Homework

What Is the Theory of Multiple Creative Abilities?

Teacher: Can't you come up with a better excuse than the dog
ate my homework?

Student: OK, the Chupacabra ate it.

—Personal anecdote told to me by a teacher

The conversation above exemplifies a student exhibiting creativity. Cheeky creativity, to be sure, but an illustration that originality can be demonstrated not just in the traditional arts but in a variety of disciplines and in real-life tasks.

Given the multitude of opportunities all of us have for exhibiting innovation, why do so many teachers think that creativity belongs only in the art room? Why do so many parents simply write creativity off as frosting on a high-brow cultural cake? Why do so many of us feel intimidated when asked if we ourselves are "creative"?

When we think about creativity as only a major cultural achievement, we assume the odds that we ourselves or our students being recognized as genuinely creative are pretty poor.

It's because we don't differentiate between Big-C and little-c creativity.

Big-C and little-c Creativity

In his book *Creativity: Flow and the Psychology of Discovery and Invention,* psychology professor Mihaly Csikszentmihalyi (1997) divides creativity into two types: big and little. Big-C creativity is that which most of us think of when we think of creative people. Those who break the norms of art like Picasso, Presley, or Tharp. Those innovative scientists like Galileo, Edison, or Einstein. Those who invent or transform technology like Ford, Bezos, and Jobs. It's those folks who influence what Csikszentmihalyi calls an entire "domain."

Some researchers believe only 30 percent of the population can be considered "intuitive types"—these big-picture thinkers who create something out of nothing. The rest of us are "sensors" whose creative ability lies in combining ideas and improving existing conditions (HuffPost, 2013).

Children, writes Csikszentmihalyi (1997), cannot be considered Big-C creative since they do not have the recognition of experts and critics of a domain who would validate this type of creative person's world-changing ability. Such a definition sets a very, very high bar for something to be considered creative. This is why, as we discuss later, in education we also need a Middle-C level of creativity.

Csikszentmihalyi also recognizes the little c of creativity—the everyday, often personal, problem solving all of us do. We are all of us little-c creative when we find that we're missing an ingredient in a recipe and need to substitute. When two of our children need to be at different places at the same time. When the lesson we planned can't be taught because the Internet is down. When we need to write something romantic in the Valentine's Day card to our sweetie and we may not be feeling especially affectionate.

We improvise.

We monitor and adjust.

We innovate like MacGyver in the old television program.

We exercise what I think of as "duct tape ingenuity."

As much as I admire the Spielbergs, the Warhols, and the Beethovens of this world, I appreciate the really good little-c creative people with whom I work every day perhaps even more. The problem solvers. The initiators. Teachers who do something a little crazy hoping the crazy thing may capture the attention of some kids who weren't engaged before. The tech who devises an ingenious work-around. The librarian who creates nonstandard library policies that treat library users as real people. The administrator who figures out a policy that makes everyone involved satisfied.

A librarian once told me that when she went to teach a lesson on Internet searching to a lab full of students, she found that the technology department had, without warning, blocked Google. Out of frustration, she asked her class of fifth-graders what she might do. One creative girl raised her hand and suggested, "Just go to google.ca instead of google.com." It worked.

We need to honor little-c creativity in our schools and classrooms—and we should be demanding our students demonstrate little-c creativity instead of relying on adults to routinely provide the solutions—to personal issues (I forgot my iPad at home), of course, but to classroom issues as well (The class regularly forgets to charge their iPads before school starts).

Couldn't we be asking our students to apply little-c creativity for these sorts of problems?

- We have only 20 books for 26 kids in the classroom.

- When school dismisses early on snow days, some kids' parents can't come to get them until regular dismissal time.

- Jerry and Raul are always arguing.

- Alysha may be getting cyberbullied.

- The chapter on the civil rights movement in the textbook is boring and possibly inaccurate.

- The librarian only lets kids check out two books at a time.

- The wireless network is slow.

- Our newest student doesn't speak English as her native tongue.

Teachers should recognize that not all forms of creativity are demonstrated through big projects with formal assessments for a grade. Thinking of creative solutions to a problem is a habit of mind, a disposition, a personality trait—an integral part of personal responsibility.

That only gets stronger with practice.

Figure 4.1

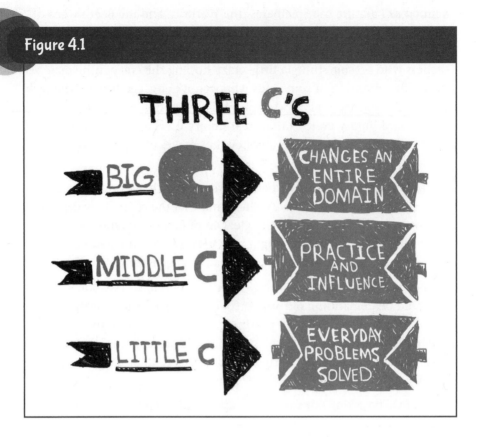

Middle-C Creativity

While students may not be able to demonstrate Big-C creativity, influencing an entire domain, they can still demonstrate originality, divergent thinking, and artistry in academic and cocurricular areas. This is Middle-C creativity. "Middle C creativity results in products appreciated in terms of interpretive skill, mastery of technical forms, distinctive style, and success in achieving a technical, practical, commercial, or academic goal" (Morelock & Feldman, 1999).

Such actions and ideas may not rise to the level of reshaping the world as we know it, but they can be significant—especially to those who exhibit such thinking. Middle-C creativity may be all that's needed to do a required academic task. It may provide practice and confidence in learners to one day attempt Big-C innovation (see Figure 4.1 above).

Most of the classroom teachers and librarians with whom I work exhibit Middle-C abilities on a daily basis. They make classrooms work because they try new things. They can think and act as situations arise that call for new ways of doing things. They modify and use technology in clever ways. They work not to change the world perhaps, but they innovate to change the world of individual children. These are great teachers who may never get a

Wikipedia entry of their own but will remain models of ingenuity to many of their students and fellow staff members.

You know who I'm talking about—possibly you.

Author's Theory of Multiple Creative Abilities

Let's examine some ways students can demonstrate these Middle-C abilities in a bit more detail.

Howard Gardner, in his 1983 book *Frames of Mind: The Theory of Multiple Intelligences,* suggested educators expand their view of intelligence. Rather than just thinking that kids who could read, write, and do math well were smart, Gardner started us considering as intelligent those children who were artistically gifted in the visual and musical arts, those who excelled physically in sports and dance, and even those who might exhibit spiritual and ecological abilities beyond the norm.

I suggest we also expand our view of creativity. While related to intelligence, creative abilities, if you remember from Chapter 2, combine the abilities to add originality to craftsmanship for effective results. Talent and giftedness are the natural ability to exhibit craft in certain areas of creativity (see Figure 4.2).

Figure 4.2

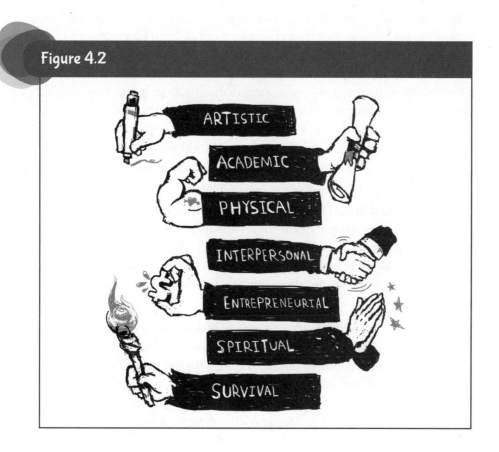

In a somewhat arbitrary fashion, I've chosen seven categories that I will call domains where I have seen students at all age levels exhibit creative abilities. And where those abilities can be practiced and honored.

1. Artistic Domain

This is the traditional area that most of us think about when we think about creativity—the arts. It's one of the big realms of Big-C creativity. It's important, perhaps not economically, but culturally.

As a former English teacher and librarian, I especially appreciate students who can demonstrate literary artistry. Personally, an eleventh-grade writing assignment I was given spurred my own interest in writing. When asked to recall an event from childhood and write about it, I chose for some reason to tell the story in the first person using the vocabulary of a younger student and made it pretty funny. Mrs. Farmer, bless her heart, shared my little paper as an example of good writing with the rest of the class. For this indifferent, lazy student, it made a huge difference.

Children by nature are born storytellers. (Sometimes it's tough to stop them.) While we can ask them to create wholly fictitious characters and events, writing in the narrative voice can also be a powerful means of sharing the results of research, experiments, or event analysis.

While the writing is still the most common academic task we ask of students, presenting is critical as well. The ability to stand in front of a group and relay ideas in a clear and compelling fashion is a lifelong skill that may be used as much, or more often, than writing. Good presentations often combine several skills with speaking—organizing, demonstrating, interacting, writing, acting, and even designing if a slideshow accompanies the talk. And the best talks are effective because they show us something we may not have seen before or seen presented in such a fashion. Paul's attempted speech on Vasco da Gama with which I started this book is a good example.

Of course, the traditional artistic forms of drawing, painting, sculpting, photography, and design have an important role in education. Giving students skills and practice in the visual arts (along with exposing them to the great works of art in history and contemporary culture) is unfortunately being relegated to the status of elective classes or dropped in elementary school programs altogether in order to provide additional time for "basic skills."

Musical artistry can be displayed in a variety of ways. Students can both sing and play musical instruments. They can compose. They can direct. They can combine music with drama to produce musical theater. Again, formal education in these areas is also being dropped in elementary schools. In middle and high schools, it has become extracurricular. While extracurricular activities are enriching and meaningful—the most meaningful parts of school for many young adults—I can't help but think we are doing a disservice to too many children by not giving them the importance these activities deserve since creativity along with skill plays an important role.

Technology is allowing students to be creative communicators in a variety of media—not just writing or face-to-face speaking. The transliterate student uses sound and visuals in new and powerful ways. Transliteracy includes the ability to take and edit still photographs; to shoot and edit video; to make audio recordings; and to use design tools to create graphics, Web pages, drawings, and charts to more clearly express ideas or explain concepts or interpret data (Thomas et al., 2007).

The importance of these creative endeavors has led to a movement to turn STEM education (an emphasis on science, technology, engineering, and math) into STEAM education with the A standing for arts. I like to think that education, the business world, and society in general all recognize that without the creativity inherent in the arts, an engineer with even the greatest craftsmanship skills and knowledge won't add much to the bottom line if she can't innovate.

2. Academic Domain

Perhaps the biggest delusion we need to dispel in education is that creativity does not play a role in the traditional academic areas of mathematics, science, and other content-specific areas. Our focus on standards, on factual knowledge, on concrete skills, and on accepted methodologies reflects the value we place on what I call *craftsmanship* in Chapter 2. Craftsmanship is vital but having it alone is not enough. Skills and knowledge not used in personal and innovative ways are just raw materials, never used to make anything of value. Such learning is not very engaging since it is not personally relevant. It is creativity within these "content areas" that has advanced civilization through new technologies, new forms of government, and new views of social justice.

Our nearly ubiquitous connection to Google, Wikipedia, and YouTube has many thoughtful educational reformers asking the value of the memorization of factual information. Do students really need to know all the state capitals when a two-second search can accurately produce that data? Do I need to know how to create a bibliographic citation when an Internet tool will do it for me? Do we need to spend time teaching (usually quite ineffectively) vocabulary lists when tapping an unknown word in an e-book displays the definition? Might our time be better spent teaching good search strategies, effective means of evaluating the quality of found information, and efforts in getting students to apply such information to genuine problems? To make meaning rather than simply acquire answers needed to pass a soon-to-be forgotten multiple-guess test? Shouldn't all tests really be open book? Or make that, connected device?

There are a number of specific areas in which we need to introduce creativity in thinking and problem solving. I single these out because of the strictness of their disciplines.

One is math and numeric problem solving. From learning basic addition and subtraction to calculus, mathematics has traditionally had a rigid set of skills. The problem, mathematically speaking, is right or wrong with no shades of gray. Hey, three plus three should always add up to six and the square of the hypotenuse is always going to equal the sum of the other two sides, right? Maybe we don't really want ingenious math students—my experience is that number facts trumps numeracy in many school's curricula.

Coding and computer programming, which I see as highly related to mathematics, are similar. The program will not run if the commands are not properly sequenced.

Yet students can develop creativity in solving numerical problems. Chances are the answer can still be judged as accurate or valid, but how one chooses to arrive at that answer may be both personal and creative. Emphasis on math applications, a solid trend among innovative math teachers, holds the key to allowing innovative approaches to math. Knowing how to calculate the area of a rectangle may be basic and needed; knowing how that knowledge can be used to determine how much paint to purchase in painting your house just might require ingenuity as well. The application of math to real-world problems (What would the impact of a rainfall deficit have on the local economy?) allows creativity, brings relevance to abstract concepts, and helps make people *numerate*—knowing how not just to do simple operations, but also to use mathematics to understand the world.

Our science classes have also emphasized the need to know a concrete body of factual information. Good that most of us can differentiate living from nonliving objects. (Although, I stumped one first-grade class when I asked them to categorize a plastic plant in their classroom.) Good chemists need to know the difference between metals and nonmetals, good physicists must understand physical laws, and astronomers ought to be able to tell you how a comet and meteor differ.

But as with math, these principles, definitions, and understanding need to be accompanied by the creative real-world applications of them—and innovative teaching methods that make them meaningful.

A popular T-shirt slogan reads "Well, another day has passed and I haven't used algebra once." While such witticisms are good for a chuckle, they hint at a real problem in today's educational system: that 90 percent of students say they are not planning on careers that involve science, technology, engineering, or math (New York Times Editorial Board, 2013).

While I love history, I have always been glad I am not a history teacher. My definition of a good teacher is primarily one who can convince students that what she has to teach has value. And for many of us, that value needs to be quite pragmatic rather than abstract. I do believe I better understand the world knowing something about the people and events of the past, but I've never been convinced by a teacher that that information helps me in any way, shape, or form in my day-to-day life. Maybe it makes me a better Trivial Pursuit player, but there is something about *trivial* in the title that bothers me. I can lump the study of literature, geography, and world languages into the same nice-to-know-but-why category.

I am certainly not arguing that we stop teaching these subjects. But such instruction needs to go beyond reading the text, listening to the lecture, and passing the exam by memorizing facts.

The best teachers in these areas that I know find ways to link what they teach to current events and children's own lives. And this gives students an avenue to demonstrate both creative interpretation and creative communications. How was the collapse of the Roman Empire like and unlike the United States today and are there lessons we should learn from the era that might solve our own country's problems? How did the ideas of Mahatma Gandhi impact India and do I agree or disagree with them—and apply them? By reading Anne Frank's *The Diary of a Young Girl,* do I better understand the plight of European Jews during World War II and are there any groups today that face the same situation?

Without relevance and the ability to work with it personally and creatively, any subject will become simply an academic hurdle kids will need to jump and as quickly as possible put behind them.

3. Physical Domain

Children and young adults can display creativity with their bodies as well as their minds. And I'm not just talking about facial piercings and tattoos. Happily, kinesthetic talents are widely appreciated and admired in our modern culture. Movie stars, professional athletes, and singers who not just belt out the tunes but shake their booties in interesting ways do not just display talent, but physical creativity as well.

Sports sometimes seem to have an inordinately important place in our current educational systems—and not just in Texas. The recognition of talented athletes in major sports is a given. What may not be a given is just how much latitude they are given to innovate—designing new plays, new team combinations, or nontraditional skills. The Fosbury Flop of the 1968 Olympics is a classic example (International Olympic Committee, 2014).

I'd add dance, of course, to the areas where Middle-C creativity can be expressed physically. Whether ballet, folk dance, or ballroom, dance brings Art with a capital *A* to movement. And while dramatics blends speaking, literature, and sometimes music, I considered it basically in the realm of physical ability. Good actors bring originality to roles they play. Often the more creative (although sometimes nuanced) the performance, the higher the accolades—and that's true both for Oscar winners and the all-school play.

4. Interpersonal Domain

As I stated at the beginning of this chapter, I truly appreciate the people with whom I work who display little-c problem-solving creativity on a regular basis. An elegant solution to a sticky problem of people or technology is in a real way as or more original than a Shakespearean sonnet.

Many students demonstrate innovation in interpersonal situations. Some students are naturally popular because they seem to be friends with everyone in the school. They've discovered ways to relate to multiple personality types with a range of values and interests.

Given the opportunity, children are great managers of learning groups and project teams. Recognizing and making the most of others' natural abilities helps them create synergies in the team. Sadly, too many adults see their role as directing these groups rather than having them be self-directed—and opening the opportunity for students to ingeniously solve their own problems.

One of the most humbling experiences I've had as an educator was finding out students are far better at creating classroom rules, library policies, and group norms than I was at devising such guidelines myself. Stuff that didn't matter to me mattered to them. And stuff that mattered to me, they rightfully thought unimportant. At a technology advisory committee meeting, the adults were considering a ban on digital audio players/recorders in school, when one brave student told of his use of his MP3 player. He used the device to record his teachers' instructions, to review his French vocabulary word list, and to tune out distractions in sometimes noisy study halls. The committee decided against the ban on such technologies. When one teacher asked students for rules concerning having personal phones in class, they all agreed that if they had them, they had to always be visible on their desktops. Creative solution, indeed!

Whether running for class president or volunteering to head a food-drive service project, students can show an uncanny ability to motivate and inspire others. A student in one of our high schools actively led a movement to have disposable foam plates and eating utensils, since he felt it was more environmentally friendly. The effort was successful over the protests of our fiscally driven food service director.

A common element among those who demonstrate interpersonal creativity is often humor. Perhaps this ability belongs in several categories of Middle-C creativity—including writing, artistry, and performance—but the juxtaposition of unrelated ideas, the surprising use of words (A man walked into bar. He said "Ouch."), and the ability to acknowledge the absurdity of a situation are the hallmarks of humor. While we as adults may be bothered by class clowns, we need to admit they are often bright, are good leaders, and probably have a bright future when they can apply humorous creativity to real problems. I like to think my personal experience as class clown now brightens dull staff meetings and workshops. The ability to laugh at oneself is to me a critical component of grit.

5. Entrepreneurial Domain

We all know kids who know how to make money. They're the lawnmowers, snow shovelers, and babysitters. Such students sell corsages at prom time or provide access to illicit products to other students. It's those kids who naturally organize the bake sales or carwashes needed to fund the Spanish club's trip to Mexico City. Many students show their civic mindedness through food drives and other charitable enterprises.

Good business and technology education programs understand what an important mindset entrepreneurship is.

Entrepreneurs look for unfilled needs and opportunities within an organization or within society—and find ways to fill them. They are self-motivated and often mission driven, traditionally creating their own businesses or products. Increasingly, the concepts of entrepreneurship apply to individuals within organizations (intrapreneurship) as well. This means looking for internal opportunities and developing skills that will keep a person and his position from becoming obsolete.

Traditionally, service organizations and business education clubs like DECA use and develop the entrepreneurial creativity in students. But I am wondering if it is time all classes in some way embrace the philosophy and offer such opportunities. Entrepreneurs need courage, tenacity, innovation, and empathy. But I am guessing they won't develop that spirit because they read the textbook from cover to cover. However, if they created and marketed a textbook . . .

6. Spiritual Domain

We know children who are very self-aware. Who connect deeply with a poem or a cause. Who may fervently believe in a religion's precepts or who seem to have developed their own set of moral principles. These abilities I'm labeling *spiritual*. Our most revered religious leaders are Big-C creatives in this realm.

Public schools have always had to walk a fine line when it comes to "teaching values" given our culture's diversity of beliefs and the belief that a free society allows its citizens to practice them as they choose. That's the theory anyway—and subject to multiple interpretations.

However, schools have traditionally had the societal charge to teach and reinforce some moral values, especially those directly related to citizenship and school behaviors. Currently, digital citizenship, using online resources safely and appropriately, is understood to be both appropriate and necessary. Federal technology funding depends on online safety curriculum being in place. Will ingenuity and creativity play a part in teaching our children how to keep from harming others and how to keep from being harmed themselves in the brave new-ish world of the Internet?

Developing creativity in spiritual beliefs and values seems a risky undertaking for schools for many reasons. But I do believe that education must recognize that asking students to think deeply about moral beliefs—especially as applied to societal conditions—is an opportunity to encourage divergent thinking.

7. Academic Survival

I've saved this one for last since it is probably the one in which I've demonstrated the greatest personal level of creativity. *Academic survival* is a nice name for the ability to make excuses, manipulate adults, and cheat without being detected.

Harvard Business School's Francesca Gino has found that cheating and creative thinking are often actually found together. "Being creative requires thinking outside the box. That's a hard thing to do when you play entirely by the rules, be they rules of society, the legal system, or even a corporate ethics handbook" (Ferro, 2014).

Children (and adults) who know all the shortcuts are often highly attuned to what tasks are worth doing and believe school work not worth doing is not worth spending a lot of time doing well. My personal First Law of School Work is this: *A job not worth doing is not worth doing well.*

To an extent, we've brought this on ourselves as educators.

Many students in all socioeconomic groups have schedules nearly as hectic and stressful as our own. Homework, sports, activities, jobs, and family responsibilities make time a precious commodity for students—especially it seems for the strivers. I offer this in the defense of creative shortcut takers.

When the assignments teachers give ask for no originality, require no higher-level thinking skills, and make no attempt to be relevant to students' lives, I would posit that educators share a portion of the blame for plagiarism and other forms of cheating. Projects and assignments that only reach Bloom's levels of remembering and understanding are often viewed by students as jobs not worth doing. Given the time constraints of many kids, who can really blame them for applying assignment triage to their homework?

And it is *our* ethical failing if our assignments do not help students learn necessary academic skills and necessary lifelong skills because they copy or find other ways to complete a valueless assignment in a minimum amount of time.

I'm not saying creativity in academic survival skills should be encouraged. But we need to recognize it exists—and perhaps can be channeled in more productive ways.

Some people, including children, may be just plain unmotivated. I know. I am one. But I would be willing to bet that far more kids we categorize as lazy are simply apathetic about the work they are asked to do—and, when given a spark of relevance and a chance to be creativity, will apply themselves.

Regardless of the subject we teach, we have an obligation to help students develop their creative capacity. It's not just the art teacher's job.

Up for Discussion

1. Do Csikszentmihalyi's Big-C versus little-c definitions of creativity make sense for education? Does only acknowledging creativity when it is Big-C encourage or discourage teachers' attempts to foster it in students? Does education need to also allow for Middle-C creativity?

2. Give an example of little-c creativity you or a colleague have recently exhibited. Do we do enough to encourage students to exhibit real-world innovation?

3. Are there categories of creativity which should be added to this book's list of seven?

4. Are there situations when creative academic shortcut taking should be rewarded?

A Job Not Worth Doing Is Not Worth Doing Well

What Are the Attributes of Projects That Help Instill Creativity?

1. What do you love?

2. What are you good at?

3. What do you want to change?

—Google (2014)

Google's online Science Fair program asks students to consider the three questions above when choosing a project. The science fair's judging criteria include

- **Inspirational** entry or idea—does it really stand out?

- Capacity to **make an impact**—could the science demonstrated make a difference to the world around us?

- **Passion** for science—would you be a good role model for other young scientists?

- **Excellence** of method—have you demonstrated real skill in their science/engineering planning and implementation of their experiment(s)?

- **Communication skills**—enthusiasm, clarity, confidence, effective use of media, diagrams, and Google tools.

Google, I like these questions and criteria. But for a company known for innovation, why are you not asking for creativity as well?

Project-Based Learning as Formative Rather Than Summative Assessment

In your daily work, do you take tests or complete projects?

My job as a technology director is primarily a string of projects that either I complete and manage or help my staff complete and manage successfully. Deploying student devices is a project. Implementing and maintaining networks, servers, and resources like GoogleApps for Education are projects. Planning and delivering effective professional development activities are projects. I could list dozens more, but you get the idea. Chances are your job could be viewed as a series of interrelated projects as well.

The last time I took a "test" was when I became "Google Certified." It meant reading a series of online guides on things like Gmail and GoogleSites and then passing self-administered multiple-guess quizzes at the end of each one. I studied hard for the first quiz, passed it, and realized that these were "open book" quizzes during which I could look up an answer (How much storage space does each personal user get in Google Drive?) if I was stumped.

There are two ways to view my look-up-the-answer method of test taking. It was flat out cheating or Google was testing my ability to efficiently locate the "right answer" since these were timed tests. I choose to believe the second since as fast as Google products change—often several times a month—any memorized answer might soon be inaccurate.

Some of us, of course, need to take exams for getting or renewing specialized certifications or licenses: CPR, hazardous waste management, or driver's licenses, for example.

But most of us spend our days as project-based learners and managers. Those real-world skills are why we should ask students to complete a lot of projects.

Elements of Projects That Encourage Creativity

The quality and effectiveness of school projects differ vastly. Consider the last time you visited an elementary school science fair. How many of the projects would be considered high quality using Google's criteria above? I bet the volcano model and the plant nutrient experiment wouldn't pass muster. Does making a volcano out of papier-mâché demonstrate the scientific method? Did the child who tries different fertilizers on a plant have a passion for horticulture?

I've been thinking and writing about how we can improve the quality of projects for a long time. What separates a project that falls flat, that results too often in plagiarism or paraphrasing, that kids struggle with from those that engage students, that teach important skills and concepts, and that result in real learning? That allow students to create and innovate? That are more likely to be done by students themselves rather than by their parents?

Unfortunately, I've seen too many teachers attend a conference or workshop and hear another teacher describe in exquisite, step-by-step detail, the wonderful project she does with her students. But when the teacher returns and tries the project himself, it's a dud. Was the first teacher a fraud? I doubt it.

What has happened in this type of professional learning about a successful teaching strategy is that it's fallen prey to what I call *the franchise syndrome*. Despite the fact that there are many, many wonderful independent restaurants doing quite well, very few franchise successfully. And the reason, I believe, is that while the menu, decor, and recipes can be duplicated, the passion of the individual restaurateur cannot be.

The same holds true for trying to duplicate successful projects. No matter how detailed the recipes for success, unless a teacher is passionate about the topic and pedagogy, it may well not be successful.

So instead of a dozen examples of wonderful projects, let's look at just two projects that have the potential of releasing a creative spark or two as well respect craftsmanship and see if we can extrapolate some of the elements that made them effective. If we can find those elements, we can apply them to any subject about which we're passionate.

Project One: Learning About Shapes

Ms. Hanson's math curriculum requires students be able to recognize standard geometric shapes: squares, rectangles, circles, ovals, and triangles. While worksheets and computer games have helped her students do this in the past, she decided that for too many students this knowledge is simply an abstract concept that has little relationship to the real world.

Since she now has a cart of tablet computers available to her, she decides to use the cameras in them to help students relate their math studies to their lives. Over the course of a week, Ms. Hanson sends these devices home with her students asking each of them to find and photograph ten shapes they find in nature, in buildings, and in objects in their homes.

Once the photographs have been taken, students import them into a drawing program in which they use the tools to outline the shapes they've found with bold colorful lines. The tech integration specialist was in the lab helping on the days this was done. Students use a short checklist to make sure they have completed all parts of the project. One of the criteria is to find an unusual shape and give it its own name.

When complete, Ms. Hanson has a short conference with each student about the assignment—what they learned, where they had problems, and how this information might be useful to them. The short checklist of requirements was used as part of the interview. When students failed to complete any of the requirements, she made arrangements for them to get extra help or practice.

Prints of both the original photograph and modified photographs were displayed in the classroom and online for parents and other students to review.

On reflection, Ms. Hanson saw an unusually high level of motivation to complete the project, that a higher percentage of students mastered the math concepts, and that both she and her students had fun. She's writing a grant for her own set of five classroom tablets for next year and decides to start looking for a better graphics program for use with the project.

Project Two: Oral Histories of the Civil Rights Movement

Mr. Chaves has a state standard that requires students demonstrate an understanding of the civil rights movement of the 1960s. When he has taught it in the past using a textbook and films, he finds that his students are uninterested in this piece of "ancient history," often do poorly on the unit exam, and cannot recall any significant events or lessons only a few weeks after the unit has ended.

So with the help of his librarian, he decides to change the unit up, asking students to demonstrate their learning by creating oral histories of local people who remember the 1960s.

Assigning students to groups he believes have a variety of skills, he gives them these guidelines and a rubric on which the project will be assessed:

> *You and your team must find a relative, friend, or neighbor who remembers life in the 1960s and is willing to share his or her remembrances of that time. While there are no specific questions you need to ask, your goal is to see if they can tell you about how minority groups may have been treated differently during that time compared with today. You may choose to record their recollections as a sound recording, on video, or in writing.*
>
> *You will also need to select one other secondary source of information about the era—a textbook chapter, a book, or a documentary—and compare and contrast it with the oral history of the person you*

*interviewed. Try to answer this question: Did the civil rights movement of
the 1960s have a lasting impact? If you feel you have a more significant
question about the era, that's great—but talk to me about it first.*

*You may choose how to present your findings. You may give an oral report
accompanied by a computer slideshow, create a video, or write a paper.
Exemplary presentations will be original and creative. All reports will be
shared online with the school and the interviewees. A short written personal
reflection on what you learned is also required. This will not be shared.*

*Mr. Chavez spent time in class helping students establish group norms, determine
job responsibilities, and develop a timeline to organize task completion deadlines.
He also encouraged groups to develop their own quality criteria for the completed
work—and to think creatively about their conclusion and presentation.*

*At the end of the unit, Mr. Chavez reviewed each project and his own effort. He
observed that students were more engaged, demonstrated high-order thinking, and
some students showed creativity both in their conclusions and how they
communicated their findings. He determined the rubric needed to be clearer and
some students needed extra help from the librarian in creating good videos and
finding secondary sources. A short student survey of the project revealed that while
students found the project challenging, they liked the personal relationships they
formed with interviewees and were proud of their finished product.*

While these assignments have different educational objectives and are
done with very different age groups, both have some common elements
that fall into three categories: assignments, activities, and assessments (see
Figure 5.1).

Assignments that matter to the student include

1. **Projects that allow creativity have clarity of purpose
   and expectations.** As I wrote earlier, good teachers make sure
   students know "why" the subject is important. Ms. Hanson told
   students that being able to describe objects in geometric terms
   everyone agrees on will be useful all their lives. (I'd like to buy an
   oval table, please.) Mr. Chavez knew that some of his minority
   students are still impacted by societal discrimination and they
   need to know that discrimination is something that can be
   mitigated politically. Checklists and rubrics of expected quality
   criteria were given at the beginning of these assignments.
   Students knew exactly what each teacher expected them to do.
   Each tool, however, encouraged students to think creatively.
   Models of past projects, both good and bad, can provide an
   excellent focus for discussion on the qualities of an effective
   final product.

Figure 5.1

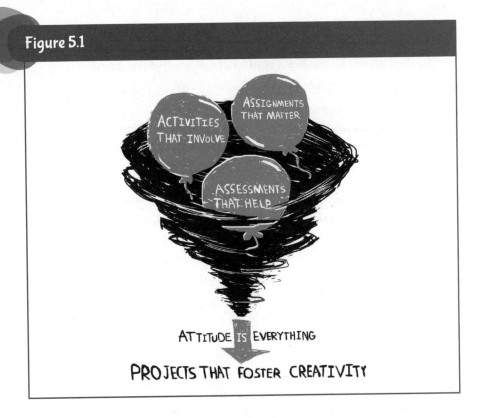

2. **Projects that allow creativity give students choices.** If the purpose of the assignment is to teach a basic understanding (how past events impact our lives today) or a set of skills (being able to recognize a geometric shape), it doesn't make any difference what the example might be. If a student takes a picture of a toy with a circular design or a tree stump, does it matter? Dig down and look at the core concepts that projects are trying to teach and let the students pick specific subjects that interest them.

3. **Projects that allow creativity are relevant to the student's life.** For today's students, Dr. Martin Luther King Jr. marching on Washington is about as real as George Washington crossing the Delaware. But by asking his students to interview their families or members of the community, Mr. Chavez added real faces and lives to these events. The stories resonated with those doing the interviewing. By taking photos of their environment, students learn geometric shapes exist in their own lives. So many times we ask our students to research important topics—environmental, historical, or social issues—but fail to help them make the vital connection of why the findings are important to today. Strive for projects that are relevant because they are timely, local, or personal.

4. **Projects that allow creativity stress higher-level thinking skills and innovation.** Think how different the results of a project that asks for a creative solution to a problem are from a paper that simply asks an "about" question. (List ten facts "about" the role of the church in the civil rights movement.) Find ways to move up Bloom's taxonomy from the Understanding level to Analyzing, Evaluating, and Creating. ("What are the three most common geometric shapes you found in your house? Why do you think that might be?) If a teacher doesn't ask for originality, the best they're going to get is creative paraphrasing.

5. **Projects that allow creativity answer genuine questions.** At the beginning of the project, most students didn't know the impact the civil rights movement may have had on members of their community. Mr. Chavez probably didn't know these things either. Ms. Hanson didn't know what children might photograph as an example of a triangle. Genuine questions are ones to which the teacher does not have a preconceived answer. Unfortunately, adults rarely ask questions to which they do not believe they already know the answer. Good projects try to answer only genuine questions. As a side benefit, unexpected products are a whole lot more interesting for the teacher to read or view too.

Activities that involve the student include

6. **Projects that allow creativity involve a variety of information finding activities.** As teachers and librarians, we are comfortable with our familiar primary sources of reference books, textbooks, periodicals, and trade books. Yet the answers to many personal, local, and timely questions cannot be found in them. While they can provide excellent background information of important facts, we often need to talk to experts, conduct surveys, design experiments, or look at other kinds of primary sources to get precise information. The learners in these examples spent time with secondary sources, but the generation of new knowledge and creative perspectives came from interviews and original photographs.

7. **Projects that allow creativity are hands on.** Students in the examples above conducted interviews, did online searches, created presentations and photographs, and gave oral presentations. Mr. Chavez's students used cameras to take photographs and videos to be used within the slideshows. Ms. Hanson's students used tablets to take photos. They learned how to upload and modify photographs. Students were learning by

doing, not just listening. Notice, too, how many corollary skills are practiced in these projects: interpersonal skills, writing skills, interviewing skills, photography skills, layout and design skills, and speaking skills.

8. **Projects that allow creativity use technology in productive ways.** Whether for planning, for research, or for communication, most students find the use of technology motivating. The students in the examples used computer programs that were *not* purposely designed to be "motivational." It is the challenge of creating original content and designing containers for that content that give good productivity tools like cameras, recording equipment, graphic programs, slideshow creators, and Web page construction kits—the virtual equivalent of a set of LEGOs—their motivating qualities. And of course, open doors for original uses.

9. **Projects that allow creativity use formats that take advantage of multiple senses.** Mr. Chavez's students were asked to communicate their finds not only with words, but sound and sight as well. Our ability to digitize and present information is no longer restricted to the written word but now can include drawings, photos, sounds, music, animations, and movies. All are formats that carry important and often unique information in possibly innovative ways. By asking that information be presented in more ways than writing or speaking, the "intelligences" of a larger percent of the class can be harnessed and validated. While I can write, I think I'd want team members with good interpersonal and design skills on my team doing oral histories.

10. **Projects that allow creativity are often complex but are broken into manageable steps.** One of the first things Mr. Chavez helped his students do was outline the tasks to be done and establish a timeline for their completion. Checking off completed tasks is satisfying, and students learned some corollary planning and time management skills in the process. Large projects can be overwhelming even for adults, but planning smaller steps, building timelines, creating frequent deadlines, and scheduling multiple conferences turn complexity into manageability. This task chunking for many of us makes us "grittier," a disposition critical to creative success as we learned in Chapter 2. It's also clear that some tasks in effective projects often require sustained periods of time to complete. In an overloaded curriculum, this can be problematic, leading to the Platte River courses that are a mile wide and only an inch deep. We should ask if one effective teaching

strategy—project-based learning—might be less time consuming than reteaching standards, year after year, through more traditional methods.

11. **Projects that allow creativity can be collaborative and result in better products than individual work.** Mr. Chavez asked his students to work in teams. Joint problem solving, assigning and accepting responsibility, and discovering and honoring individual talents help create a synergy that resulted in better, more satisfying products than students working alone would have produced. Not every project needs to be a joint effort, but real-world work environments increasingly stress teamwork. Teamwork in school is not only more enjoyable but also gives students the opportunity to practice creativity in the interpersonal domain. Remember that students can show creativity in interpersonal tasks.

Assessments that help the learner include

12. **Projects that allow creativity have results that are shared with people who care and respond.** Mr. Chavez's kids got the same credit as those who may have simply taken a multiple-choice test or written a short paper on the civil rights movement. So why would kids go to all the extra work on a project like the one described entails? Kids get hooked because adults take the time to really look at the work they have done and comment on it. The community, both physically and virtually, could view the student's online presentations and leave comments—both compliments and criticisms. Ms. Hanson's students knew their parents would see their work during open house or parent-teacher conferences as well as online. Assessments and reviews by peers, experts, and neighbors (any audience beyond the teacher) are common in scouting, athletics, dramatics, 4-H, and music groups. Students who know they have a public audience tend to have a higher degree of concern about the quality of their work. Let's face it, some kids just don't care what the teacher thinks.

13. **Projects that allow creativity are assessed by an authentic tool rather than a paper and pencil test.** Students had the checklists and rubrics at the beginning of the project and used them several times to determine their progress during the project. It was easy to recognize both what was completed as well as what needed improvement. These tools provide an effective means of doing formative assessments. When students are given quality indicators like these at the beginning rather than end of the assignment, they

can use them to guide their learning and keep guesswork to a minimum. When shared, parents can become partners by doing quality control. As students become more sophisticated in the assessment process, they should be expected to choose or design their own "quality indicators"—one of the attributes of a genuinely creative person.

14. **Projects that allow creativity ask the learner to reflect, revisit, revise, and improve their final projects.** Ms. Hanson's individual conferences asked even her young students to reflect on the project—what they learned and still needed to practice. While Mr. Chavez's class had a completion date, students continued to edit and revise their work as they received feedback from website visitors and their peers. For many students, this project became a part of their digital portfolio of work. There is satisfaction to be gained from observed growth. Creative works, such as gardens, musical repertoires, and relationships, are always works in progress.

Why don't all teachers design projects with some or all of these elements. Well, a fourth *A* sneaks in.

Attitude is everything:

15. **Teachers who enjoy authentic, project-based learning in which creativity is encouraged are comfortable with a loss of control over time, the final product, and "correct" answers.** If some parts of the curriculum don't get covered, if conflicting evidence causes confusion, or a controversial solution to a problem is suggested, these educators roll with the punches. They have the intellectual confidence to handle ambiguity.

16. **These teachers and librarians enjoy active students rather than passive students.** They have developed new rules of behavior that stress student responsibility and have trained their principals to differentiate between active learning and students out of control. Doing rather than memorizing involves movement and noise.

17. **The professional's belief that given enough time, resources, and motivation, all students are capable of high performance is critical.** It's not just the talented and gifted student who can make choices, solve problems creatively, and complete complex tasks. These teachers and librarians know that all

students rise to the level of performance expected of them, that great ideas can come from anyone in the class, and that all students can have original ideas and execute them. It's formative assessment that recognizes time, not native ability, is variable in student achievement.

18. **Teachers who do exciting projects recognize that their expertise is in the learning process, information literacy, and creativity development rather than in any particular subject area.** No longer is the primary role of the educator that of information dispenser, but of guide for information users and creators. The sage-on-the-stage is being overshadowed by the video-on-YouTube. The happiest teachers are colearners in the classroom, especially when learning new technology tools. And students get the satisfaction that comes from teaching as well.

19. **Teacher enthusiasm becomes more important than ever.** The best projects are designed by teachers who are enthusiastic about what they are doing and how they are doing it. They are personally excited about their subjects and believe deeply students need to know what they have to teach. The downside to this is that it is very difficult to create recipes for specific projects that can be easily adopted by other teachers. We can all use principles and guidelines like the ones in this chapter, but to say a project, no matter how well designed, is going to work for every teacher or every group of students is impossible.

20. **Teachers who work on these kinds of projects know that they don't always work the first time.** But they keep trying. These teachers display grit as well.

Projects must matter. The task needs to be important to the researcher and allow the researcher latitude for original ideas and approaches to gathering, interpreting, and communicating it. If it isn't, students will go through the motions. And remember my First Law of School Work will kick in: *A job not worth doing is not worth doing well.* One of the best things teachers can do is work very hard to make sure research projects are well designed and intrinsically motivating.

Ask yourself if the quality of your project level is of importance to the student and capacity for creative work. Every project should be at Level Three. Fortunate students will get to do Level Four tasks during their school years that will build their sense of empowerment and confidence in their own creativity.

Level	Attributes	Primary Example	Secondary Example
One	The project is about a broad topic. Students can complete the assignment by using a general reference source such as an encyclopedia or Wikipedia. Students cannot make a connection between the project and their daily lives. Creativity is not asked for or encouraged.	My project is about a disease.	My project is about a career.
Two	The project answers a question that helps students narrow the focus of information gathering. This question will require various sources of information in order to get a reliable answer. To complete the project, the students will need to clearly state a supported answer to the question. While a creative answer may be possible, the project focuses in factual information.	What are the most common symptoms of the disease?	Is the career I am studying one that is more likely to add or lose jobs in the future?
Three	The project requires students to answer questions or solve problems of personal relevance. To answer these questions, students will need to use primary sources of information (original surveys, interviews, source documents) as well as secondary sources (magazines, newspapers, books, or the Internet). Higher-level thinking skills, including creativity, will need to be demonstrated to successfully complete these projects.	What disease might I be likely to contract based on my family's medical history?	Based on my personal interests and academic strengths, what are the top three careers I should consider pursuing?
Four	The project requires students to answer questions or solve problems of a personal relevance but also contains information that can be used by decision makers as they make policy or distribute funds. The result of the project is a well-supported argument that includes an innovative call for action on the part of an organization or government body along with a plan to share or distribute this information.	How can my family and I reduce the chances of contracting my disease through lifestyle changes?	How can my school change its course offerings and opportunities to help me and other students pursuing my career?

As the Buck Institute for Education (BIE; 2014), a terrific resource for educators wanting to effective means of conducting project based learning, states, "Project Based Learning's time has come. The experience of thousands of teachers across all grade levels and subject areas, backed by research, confirms that PBL is an effective and enjoyable way to learn." As BIE suggests, project-based learning requires that the content is significant, the inquiry is in depth, the work is question driven, the student has a voice in choosing the product, the work is shared with an audience beyond the classroom, and creativity and innovation are "explicitly taught and assessed."

Enjoyable learning experiences that are both motivating and meaningful don't just happen. They require thoughtful preparation and the conscious use of lessons learned from previous successful projects. All of us who work with students on projects need to keep asking ourselves questions like

1. What are the barriers to better projects?

2. How do we create meaningful assessment tools that can help us become more comfortable with ambiguity and creativity?

3. How do I make sure all students are intrinsically motivated to keep learning throughout their lives by creating, finding, evaluating, and using information?

Lifelong learning is a reality for all of us, student and educator alike.

Creativity Starts With a Personal Problem

Those who study creativity agree that most innovation is the by-product of finding a solution to a problem. The Apple II was a creative solution to making a computer that was affordable and easy to use. Third-way thinking is the creative solution to resolving political disagreements. *Game of Thrones* is a creative means of providing entertainment to millions of people. "How shall I love thee, let me count the ways" may have been a creative way to win the heart of a lover and express an inexpressible emotion. If you think about it, nearly every technology or technical improvement, every work of art, every new strategy in a sport, or any new theory of success, health, or happiness is the result of unmet needs and previously unsolved problems.

The term *personalized education* is getting a foothold in education. Differentiated instruction treats subgroups of students in different ways. Individualized education treats individuals in different ways. But personalized education asks that we not only treat each student as an individual, but also as a unique being with unique sets of interests and abilities. And we teach those students by linking their learning to those interests and abilities.

When I was a librarian, I once had an eighth-grade student in my school who loved horses. She insisted we get a horse magazine and horse books for the library. Every picture she drew in her notebook was of horses. She spent her time outside of school caring for her horse, on 4-H projects involving her horse, and riding in horsey sorts of competitions.

Unfortunately, her history teacher wanted a research paper done on World War II.

As it happened, I had watched a documentary on WWII just before this assignment was given and I noticed that the German army used a lot of horses to pull equipment from battlefield to battlefield. While we all know about the Panzers and other technologies of this war, horses were still being used extensively.

So just off the top of my head, I suggested to my little horse lover that she use "What role did horses play in the battles of WWII?" as her guiding question. And it actually worked. It helped her narrow the focus of her paper as well as got her interested in WWII as a historical event by giving the assignment relevance to her. The lesson I learned as an educator is that it is possible and useful to blend students' personal interests with academic standards.

Projects that have the greatest chance of bringing out creative results in students will be those that help students solve personal or personally interesting problems.

Up for Discussion

1. How can creativity become a more integral part of project-based learning?

2. Is personalizing education a realistic strategy for teacher who may see 150 students a day?

3. The BIE website stated that project-based learning allows teachers to "rediscover the joy of learning alongside their students." Is this a realistic expectation? Might creativity play a part in this rediscovery?

4. What other elements should be added to the four A's that may increase the likelihood of a student demonstrating creativity? Are some elements more important than others?

5. Revise an "about" assignment ("Write a paper about a career.") to bring it to Level Three or Level Four in this chapter's rubric. Is moving to these levels difficult, and if so, why?

List Three Right Answers

What Are Some Simple Ways Teachers Can Promote Creative Thinking Every Day?

Everyone is born creative; everyone is given a box of crayons in kindergarten. Then when you hit puberty they take the crayons away and replace them with dry, uninspiring books on algebra, history, etc. Being suddenly hit years later with the "creative bug" is just a wee voice telling you, "I'd like my crayons back, please."

—Hugh MacLeod (2009)

I hope you are not looking for formulas. Or handouts. Or a single technique. Or even a "method." The creativity-inspiring classroom is a culture—not a set of rules or specific activities. It is a mindset that teachers transfer to their students *every* day.

Quite honestly, I don't know if creativity can be taught. But I know that creativity doesn't just happen. It needs to be cultivated by being

- Allowed
- Encouraged
- Displayed
- Modeled
- Recognized and rewarded
- Developed
- Discussed

But directly taught as a separate skill? So far nothing I've read or seen allows me to believe it can or should be.

But to keep this from being a terribly short chapter, I will identify some things teachers can purposely do in their classrooms that increase the odds of both their students and themselves being more creative.

1. **Ban clip art—in all assignments.** I know, I know—clip art is quick, easy, and readily available in many programs. But don't let kids use it. They should be creating their own visuals for their projects. Scanned original drawings, illustrations created with graphics programs, and personally taken and edited photographs are all ready sources of visual information we haven't all seen dozens of times. Let's put those cameras, drawing programs, graphics tools, and scanners to creative use. You, as the teacher, should as well.

2. **Ask for information to be shared in at least two media formats or different writing types.** Even if the primary requirement of an assignment is a piece of writing, we can ask that the same information be shown in many ways. A few I've gleaned from various sources are listed in Figures 6.1–6.4 (see pages 66–67).

   Think of all the media and styles humans use to communicate. Using multiple media and different types of written communication requires the learner to think about the contents in two different ways and encourages new approaches to delivering a message. Give kids a chance to try them all.

   In preparation for the next chapter, think about how technology can or must be used in making these things.

3. **Encourage the narrative voice in writing and oral presentations.** Good assignments help teach not just content, but learning processes as well. Ask students not just to tell the answer to a research question but to tell the story about how they found the

information, what challenges they faced, and what new tricks they acquired.

One of my favorite examples of this was told by Ken Macrorie (1988) of *I-Search* fame. He writes of a girl who was asked to write a paper on a vocation. Following the teacher's advice for getting primary information through an interview of a local expert, the girl, who was interested in becoming a firefighter, interviewed the local fire chief. He turned out to be a sexist pig. The interview made her mad, so she went to her library for secondary sources to learn all she could about the physical, emotional, and intellectual needs of good firefighters. She discovered she exhibited all of them—and delivered her information to the fire chief. And she told of her experiences as part of her final report. Now wouldn't that have been fun to read?

Make research a journey, not just a destination, and ask students to tell that story—emphasizing creative problem-solving strategies.

4. **Ask for multiple possible answers to questions or multiple possible solutions to problems.** Most adults who read the paper have political opinions or have encountered puzzling events and recognize there is rarely if ever a single viewpoint on an issue or just one solution to a problem. By asking kids for two or three "right" answers, not only do they need to be more creative, but perhaps more empathetic as well.

On trips with our grandchildren, we sometimes play card-based quiz games like Brain Buster. But we have a rule: We have to come up with a "correct" response that's not a given option and explain why it's correct. For one question, "What falls from the sky and turns the ground white?" snow was the "one-right-answer." But two little boys in back seat easily found that fruit blossoms, sleet, hail, and, of course, bird poop were also correct.

Don't just ask for multiple possible answers but ask students to rank them from best to worst and explain why they did so.

5. **Don't ask for a "right" answer.** In an interesting experiment, elementary children were shown a triangle. One group was told that if they completed the painting in "the right way" they would get a point. Another group was simple told to "complete the painting." The students who assumed there was a "right answer" drew simple houses 80 percent of the time and used an average of only two colors; the students who were not told there was a right answer created a large variety of scenes (no simple houses) and used an average of five colors (Segev, 2013). Do examples that are too explicit have this same level of inhibiting creativity as well?

Figure 6.1

ADVERTISEMENT OR BILLBOARD	DEBATE	SAYING OR PROVERB	ADVICE COLUMN
JOURNAL	SONG OR ANTHEM	POSTER	SPOOF OR PARODY
CARTOON	POLICY PAPER	LETTERS TO THE EDITOR OR EDITORIALS	DEMONSTRATION
POLITICAL CAMPAIGNS	BUSINESS PLAN	POSTCARD	VENN DIAGRAM
DRAMATIC SCRIPT	CLASS RULES	SPEECH	DIARY OF A REAL OR IMAGINARY PERSON
LEGEND OR TALL TALE	TABLE OF "ELEMENTS"	COMPUTER PROGRAM	DIORAMA

Figure 6.2

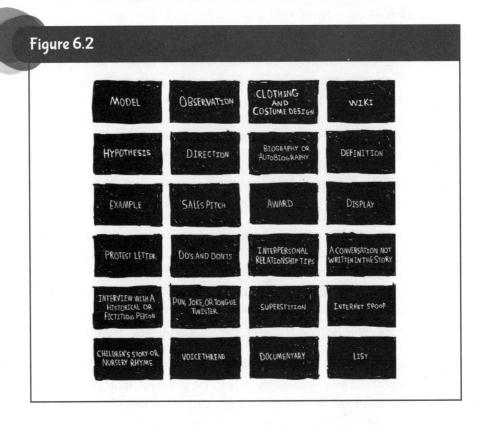

MODEL	OBSERVATION	CLOTHING AND COSTUME DESIGN	WIKI
HYPOTHESIS	DIRECTION	BIOGRAPHY OR AUTOBIOGRAPHY	DEFINITION
EXAMPLE	SALES PITCH	AWARD	DISPLAY
PROTEST LETTER	DO'S AND DON'TS	INTERPERSONAL RELATIONSHIP TIPS	A CONVERSATION NOT WRITTEN IN THE STORY
INTERVIEW WITH A HISTORICAL OR FICTITIOUS PERSON	PUN, JOKE, OR TONGUE TWISTER	SUPERSTITION	INTERNET SPOOF
CHILDREN'S STORY OR NURSERY RHYME	VOICETHREAD	DOCUMENTARY	LIST

Figure 6.3

PUPPET SHOW	LOVE NOTE, POEM, OR SONG	PUZZLE	SYMBOL
LYRICS	QUESTIONNAIRE OR SURVEY	WIKIPEDIA ENTRY	MACHINE, TOOL, OR GADGET
CONTEST	GAME	COMPUTER GAME	ELEVATOR SPEECH
PROLOGUE OR EPILOGUE	AFFIRMATION	NEWSLETTER OR MAGAZINE	PODCAST
BOOK JACKET	MAP	RANSOM NOTE	TWITTER POST
EVALUTION	REACTIONS AND REVIEW	CHECKLIST	RUBRIC

Figure 6.4

TEST OR QUIZ	LESSON	EXAGGERATION	MEMORY
RECIPE	FAN FICTION	THANK-YOU NOTE	INFOGRAPHIC
MUSIC VIDEO	PARODY	THEATER PROGRAM	BROCHURE
EXCUSE	MENU	BULLETIN BOARD	SCHOOL SIGNAGE
MASCOT	METAPHOR	NEWS STORY	NEW PLANT, ANIMAL, OR MICROORGANISM
DYSTOPIAN OR UTOPIAN WORLD	SCREENSAVER	MOTIVATIONAL SAYING	OBITUARY

6. **Give points for "design" on selected assignments.** Neatness counts. It always did and always will. But today's effective communicator needs to know some design skills as well. If you don't have them yourself, I suggest reading Robin Williams's wonderful little book *The Non-Designer's Design Book*. It takes about an hour and will change the way you look at everything you produce. In it she demonstrates four simple design rules that everyone can master—proximity, alignment, repetition, and contrast. Your own materials will look professional as well—and you can pass your secrets on to your students. And to be fair, make sure the students know that design will be considered a factor in the assessment of the product.

7. **Instead of simply telling a student the response is "wrong," ask for a reason why the answer was given.** Remember in Chapter 3 how poor George, when answering a standardized test question about what rabbits eat, had to draw in a carrot since he assumed the test creators did not know the "right" answer? By asking students why they gave the answer they did, misunderstandings can certainly be cleared up, but sometimes a refreshingly new approach to a problem emerges.

   Related to this is asking students to *show their work*. It's a term most closely associated with math problems, but we should ask for first drafts, sketches, and notes prior to accepting final products. Good teachers are as or more interested in the learning process than the final product. It's often where creative insights first appear and can give validity to an idea that only at first glimpse is "wrong."

8. **Use technologies that encourage creativity.** I've long sensed that kids like technology because its use in schools is often the only chance they get to be creative. Even if it just selecting the background of slide show or the font of a paper, kids get some choices. But in the next chapter, we'll look more closely at the rules involved in finding, selecting, and using those tools.

9. **Ask students to help formulate classroom rules, modify procedures, and solve issues.** Students can and should demonstrate their creativity in areas other than the arts. Are you having a problem writing a class rule that's needed but that everyone can't buy into? Turn the problem over to your students for their creative solutions. I did this once when I ran an unruly library. The high school students replaced my mile-long list of thou-shalt-nots with this elegant set:

To be in the library you must

Be doing something productive

Be doing it in a way that allows others to be productive

Be respectful of other people and their property

This had the added benefit of creating students who understood their actions impacted others. This is the first time I've admitted that these rules were not a product of my own genius—but those of my students.

Is there conflict or tension in your class? I'll bet you've got kids who have creative interpersonal skills who can suggest a new approach. Try it and see what happens.

10. **Honor students' personal interests and unique talents when teaching skills.** In order for students to think hard, think broadly, and think creatively about a subject, they must have enough interest in that subject to care about it. Combining a personal interest with a mandated research topic can lead to creativity. Required content + personal interest = success and originality. Remember from the previous chapter that all creativity starts with a personal problem.

11. **Honor student creativity by giving it a CC License.** Students should be required to assign a Creative Commons (CC) license to every final product that is more than clever paraphrasing or a blatant copy. The recognition that one's own work can and should be used by others in their own creative processes has given rise to a new means of intellectual property control called Creative Commons.

    The movement, cofounded by Stanford Law School professor and author Lawrence Lessig in 2001, is a backlash against what many see as overly restrictive copyright laws that keep intellectual property out of the public domain for an unreasonably long period of time. But by using a Creative Commons license, the intellectual property creator (the student) openly gives others varying degrees of rights to use the property in the belief the work can be used, changed, and improved upon by others. More importantly, it ensures that students recognize their creative works have true value.

    A side benefit of this approach also asks students to think about their own attitudes toward the copy-protected work of others. If you self-identify as a creator, you are more empathetic to the creative efforts of others and understand why piracy and plagiarism are unethical.

12. **Respect remixing.** One of the hallmarks of the net generation is their love of using two or more commercial media to create a new product. Long a staple of popular music, combining original video with a popular song is not just something done by individual students, but entire schools. (Search YouTube using the terms *high school spirit video* and you'll find dozens of examples.)

The use of copyrighted materials in student projects has been controversial. But in most instances the uses fall under educational fair use guidelines. Work can be considered fair use if it is of a "transformative" nature. In *Recut, Reframe, Recycle* (Aufderheide & Jaszi, 2008), the authors define these uses of copyrighted works in online videos as "transformative" and meeting fair use guidelines:

- Parody and satire
- Negative or critical commentary
- Positive commentary
- Quoting to trigger discussion
- Illustration or example
- Incidental use
- Personal reportage or diaries
- Archiving of vulnerable or revealing materials
- Pastiche or collage

A well-recognized form of creativity is combining two disparate ideas in original ways. Isn't this the definition of *mash-up*?

13. **Teach the proper use of quoted materials.** One of the mistakes we make in teaching copyright is that students cannot use the words of another person in their own work. While it is certainly true that other's words and work need to be attributed to the original source, quoting for purposes of definition, contrast, clarification, and other reasons can be a powerful way of getting a message across. Hey, sometimes people say something so well, it would nearly impossible to say it better. It's OK for students to recognize the creativity of others and its effectiveness—and use it to build personal products.

14. **Add creativity spaces for display of student work in your classroom.** Bulletin boards should display students' creative efforts not those of commercial artists who work for school supply companies. Your signage should be student made. How about letting your most frequent bathroom-goers design those ubiquitous passes?

Why should all school communications not be student designed? Websites, brochures, handbooks, and signage should all be done by the owners of the school—the students.

Increasingly large flat-panel monitors are used to display announcements. These tools can just as easily show photo or videos of students' creative work.

15. **Adding "makerspaces" to your classroom and library.**
Makerspaces are dedicated areas that provide workstations with fast processing speed, adequate memory, and software for video and still photo editing, music production, voice recordings, computer programming, multimedia composition, and 3-D printers. The areas often provide green screens to shoot video in front of so another background can later be added in editing.

Even in schools that are one-to-one with tablets or netbooks for all students, access to these more powerful computers is needed for tasks that need power. As libraries shift from places where information is acquired to where information is produced, they should be repurposing spaces left empty as digital materials replace physical ones.

But what about my nine-hundred-square-foot classroom? Most classrooms have at least one "student computer," if not several. Ask yourself what sort of software is available on these machines. Is it just a few educational games that entertain and drill-and-kill software that teaches some low-level basic skills or factoids, or do you give children access to productivity and creativity tools that help them produce their own work?

And primary-grade teachers, please keep your art and storytelling areas as important "makerspaces" as well. Although technology is often associated with them, makerspace is really a philosophy—"community centers with tools" (Maker Media, 2014)—and those tools can range from scissors and construction paper to sewing machines to circuit boards to CAM/CAD software.

16. **Modify your discussions to allow for divergent ideas and interests.** As we'll examine in Chapter 10, our most divergent thinkers can be the most challenging with whom to work. These are the ones who always seem to be ahead, behind, or out in left field judging by their questions and comments. One expert recommends writing these off-the-wall questions on a special place on the whiteboard and then addressing them once a week (Clifford, 2012).

17. **Discuss the creative work of experts.** Always be on the lookout for examples of ingenuity, good design, innovative ideas, and other forms of creativity and share them with your students. Some great discussion questions might be

- How is this approach like or unlike others you've seen?
- What is the original element?
- What problem does this original product attempt to solve?
- What elements of craftsmanship does it display?
- What can we learn from it?

Do you share the work of your favorite innovators—those people and organizations that consistently surprise you—with your students?

18. **Make creativity a one of the criteria on all assessments.** We'll look at this more fully in Chapter 8.

19. **Seek out the creative ideas of other educators.** Keep your eyes open for innovative and effective projects and practices of other librarians and teachers. Use others' creative approaches and make them your own. That will require a powerful professional learning community that we'll learn how to build in Chapter 9. It's not just music that can be remixed.

I am not going to number this final suggestion because it deserves special attention. We started this chapter by listing what we as educators can do about creativity. We can

- Allow it
- Encourage it
- Display it
- Model it
- Recognize and reward it
- Develop it
- Discuss it

I will add one more. We also need to

- Respect it and the students who demonstrate it

Earlier we discussed how courage is a critical attribute of the creative individual. Fear of ridicule clamps a lot of mouths from offering divergent opinions and keeps a lot of hands from designing something original. (I bet this happens in your staff meetings as well.) Research shows that "communities of creativity" are very effective in bringing out the creativity in everyone in them.

Do an honest assessment of how you personally respond to "wrong" answers, assumptions, or points of view. Are they immediately dismissed or corrected—or are they investigated? Do you yourself acknowledge that every individual has a unique set of experiences, points of view, and problems that may be reflected in his work? Do you honestly believe the old adage "there's no such thing as stupid question"? Do you always dig a little deeper before judging?

A teacher's respect and the respect she builds in her students is the most important element of a classroom that builds rather than destroys creativity.

Up for Discussion

1. Einstein is credited with this quote: "It is the supreme art of the teacher to awaken the joy in creative expression and knowledge." Would you agree or disagree with this lofty statement?

2. Reflect on teachers you have had as a student. Do some stand out as more encouraging of creativity and divergent thinking? Why?

3. How can you channel off-the-wall comments from students in your classroom without inhibiting creative thinking?

4. What are some ways you and other teachers have promoted the proper citation of materials—and encouraged students to address the intellectual property rights of their own work?

5. What are some things you do in your classroom on a daily basis that promote creativity that are not on this chapter's list of twenty ideas?

Chapter

7

Just Because It's Pretty Doesn't Mean It's Original

Does Technology Enhance or Diminish Creativity?

One might say the computer is being used to program the child. In my vision, the child programs the computer.

—Seymour Papert (1993)

When people are asked if they are "artistic," a common response is "No, I can't draw a straight line." I've often wondered what being able to draw a straight line has to do with being artistic.

Everyone reading this chapter can use a paper and pencil to draw a house.

Some might look like this (see Figure 7.1):

Figure 7.1

And some might look like this (see Figure 7.2):

Figure 7.2

Source: https://openclipart.org/detail/175864/Clipart-by-EricOrtner

I would argue that the difference does not lie in the degree of creativity these artists display, but in the level of craftsmanship they display. Neither picture includes original elements. We've all seen houses like these before.

Remember that craftsmanship is an essential component of creativity. Sometimes we don't want people to be experimental. I'd just as soon my dentist, airline pilot, tax preparer, and bridge engineers have a working knowledge and use the best practices of their profession—unless a problem demands creativity.

But here's the question I've been asking myself: When a technology allows a person to make something that looks professional without having to master any degree of craft, does that increase or decrease the likelihood of creativity?

Technology and the Illusion of Creativity

It took me under a minute and no thought whatsoever to paste some text into the online image generator Wordle and have it generate the cloud in Figure 7.3. Looks slick and like I must be a pretty talented person. I can, of course, produce the same professional-looking graphics using dozens, if not hundreds, of online tools. I can use the built-in clip art, styles, and templates in word processing or presentation tools or find them online. Do you see the same "stock image" photos in presentations given by too many keynote speakers at conferences?

Figure 7.3

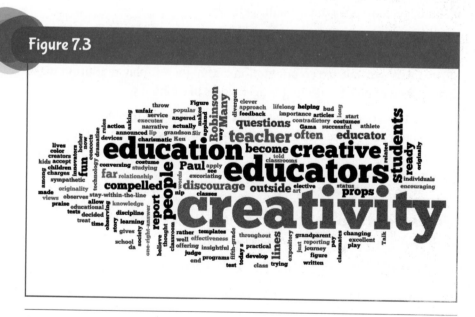

Source: Created using www.wordle.net.

These nifty new tools we teach our children to use will not guarantee they will produce a product that can be considered creative, original, innovative, or inventive.

Just because it's pretty doesn't mean it's creative.

Do Some Technologies Encourage Creativity More Than Others?

For as long as I've been a technology director, parents have been asking me about the best software to purchase for their children's use at home. Channeling Papert's observation that began this chapter, my stock answer has always been this: *Find software that allows your kids to tell the computer what to do rather than having the computer tell the child what to do.* Parents now ask me the best devices to buy for children's home use. My stock answer is similar: *Select equipment that allows your child to create, not just consume, information.* And I hint that today's information creators will need to be able to use photography, video production, sound, and graphics as well as the written word.

I've yet to see the perfect creation device on the market. While I don't really want to fan the flames of what has come down to a tablet versus laptop/ netbook war among techno-enthusiasts, I'm starting to think that one's preference may be a simple test of how one personally defines *literacy*.

At the most basic level, many adults see the need for a physical keyboard, while others see the need for a rear-facing camera. To me, if you favor a laptop, that says writing or coding is a primary skill, and if you want a tablet in your classroom, transliteracy— communicating in multiple formats including video—is a primary skill.

By virtue of screen readability, laptop fans see the ability to read short passages from a landscape-oriented screen for a short duration as literacy. Most tablets' portrait-screen orientation and higher display resolution make them a good choice for reading longer works like e-books.

We need to recognize that while neither the laptop nor the tablet is a perfect choice, both can be used in creative ways—and the key is not in the hardware. And we should recognize our own personal prejudices about what constitutes "literacy."

Show a Kid a Movie and You'll Entertain Her for an Hour; Give Her a Camera and You'll Engage Her for a Lifetime

In Chapter 1, we looked at the relationship between engagement and creativity. One of the most important aspects of engagement that differentiates it from entertainment is that the student is active rather than passive. Riffing off the old expression "give a man a fish and you feed him for a day; teach a man to fish and you feed him for a lifetime," we can also easily say, "Show a kid a movie, and you'll entertain her for an hour; give her a camera, and you'll engage her for a lifetime."

A simple way to look at technology use is to divide it into three groups: for consumption, for production, and for communication.

Consumptive uses include reading others' work, viewing images, watching videos, listening to music and spoken audio, and playing games designed primarily to be entertainment. Consumption of media is not a bad thing. We gain information and knowledge through each of these uses. Some would even argue that playing any kind of game builds grit and problem-solving skills. Each of these uses can make these devices effective babysitters as most every parent and teacher knows.

Productive technologies include writing tools, brainstorming tools, spreadsheets, databases, survey tools, video and photo editing tools, graphics creators, audio recording and editing tools, and presentation tools. Such tools that allow the products to be stored online can become wonderful ways to do formative assessments through sharing, collaborating, and peer reviewing using comments.

Communications tools and their subset of social media tools can also have educational purposes. E-mail, blogs, chat, text messaging, social photo and movie sharing (Snapchat, Vine), microblogging (Twitter), video conferencing (Skype, Google+ Hangouts, FaceTime, and probably several dozen tools kids use on a regular basis but whose existence adults are yet unaware belong in this category. There are curation tools like wikis (Wikispaces) and social bookmarking resources (Pinterest) that have social elements when shared.

Each type of tool can be used for encouraging creativity.

Technology and Bloom's Taxonomy

Several educators and organizations have attempted to categorize skills and applications according to how they might be used within Bloom's Taxonomy (Anderson & Krathwohl, 2001). I've listed them the Reference section at the end of this book.

Here is how it breaks out, starting from lower-order thinking skills to higher-order thinking skills. This list contains specific products that have stood the test of time (one or two Internet years) and that are not device specific. Most can be accessed and used with only standard Web browser. GoogleApps for Education, Office 365, and Zoho with their multiple toolsets can be used in many of these categories, so I did not list them.

This is just the tip of the iceberg, but a good place to start your personal explorations.

Level of Bloom and Associated Verbs	Technology–Aided Skills and Sample Applications
Remembering: *Recognizing, listing, describing, identifying, retrieving, naming, locating, finding, recalling* Example: Find and list five reviews of the book *The Giver* by Lois Lowry.	Curating, simple online searching, mindmapping, note-taking, bullet-pointing, highlighting, social bookmarking, favoriting **Tools:** Google search Evernote Dropbox Wikispaces
Understanding: *Interpreting, summarising, inferring, paraphrasing, classifying, categorizing, comparing, explaining, exemplifying* Example: Rank five reviews of the book *The Giver* by Lois Lowry from most positive to least positive.	Annotating, Tweeting, blogging, subscribing, advanced searching, blog journaling, tagging, commenting **Tools:** Pinterest Advanced Google Search Blogger Notability Footnote NoodleTools
Applying: *Implementing, carrying out, using, executing* Example: Interview and record a classmate who has read *The Giver.*	Interviewing, simulating, demonstrating, presenting, illustrating, running, loading, playing, operating, hacking, uploading, sharing, editing **Tools:** Coding software Scratch Google Earth Skype Big Huge Labs Motivator Screencast-o-Matic
Analyzing: *Comparing, organizing, deconstructing, attributing, outlining, finding, structuring, integrating* Example: Survey the class about their evaluation of *The Giver* and report the results in the form of a graph.	Structuring, organizing, surveying, mashing/mixing, linking, validating, reverse engineering, cracking, media clipping **Tools:** SurveyMonkey Wordle ReadWriteThink RubiStar

Level of Bloom and Associated Verbs	Technology–Aided Skills and Sample Applications
Evaluating: *Checking, hypothesizing, critiquing, experimenting, judging, testing, detecting, monitoring* Example: Share your personal review of *The Giver* with the rest of class. Invite and record reactions to the review.	Discussing, conferencing, networking, posting, collaborating, critiquing, blog commenting, reviewing, posting, moderating **Tools:** Edmodo Wikipedia GoToMeeting
Creating: *Designing, constructing, planning, producing, inventing, devising, making* Example: Create an advertisement for *The Giver*, targeting a specific demographic.	Digital storytelling, video editing, animating, podcasting, broadcasting, programming, filming, animating, blogging, publishing, videocasting, directing **Tools:** YouTube Photoshop Animoto Book Creator ToonDo Audioboom Explain Everything GarageBand iMovie Prezi GlogsterEDU VoiceThread Wet Paint 2.0

How to Evaluate an App Using the TPACK Model

I've always been distressed by the "app-happy" frenzy of many teachers and techies. Let's install every app! Let's go to every educational website! Let's assuage our FOMO (Fear Of Missing Out) and jump on board each sparkly bit of code! When I go to a conference, I want to see every "5000 Best Websites for Teachers" presentation! w00t, w00t!

I often think giving educators access to the Apple App Store is like turning kids loose in a candy shop. As of the fall of 2014, the site claims to have over 80,000 education apps available (Apple, 2014).

While I certainly appreciate teachers' enthusiasm and willingness to experiment, I wonder how many of us take the time—or have the time—to evaluate each application. Does the product teach the standards I need to have students meet? Is the game of an appropriate ability level and does it have any age restrictions? Does tutorial use good pedagogical methods? Is the tool a full-featured program or is it a teaser designed to simply sell the paid version? Does the video run on the equipment I have available? Does the tool require a login for every student? And does the program encourage the user to be creative?

While many instruments exist for software evaluation, I propose a very simple one using the TPACK technology integration model (Koehler, 2011). The author describes it as "a framework that identifies the knowledge teachers need to teach effectively with technology" and describes its three elements as "Content (CK), Pedagogy (PK), and Technology (TK)." See Figure 7.4 below.

Figure 7.4

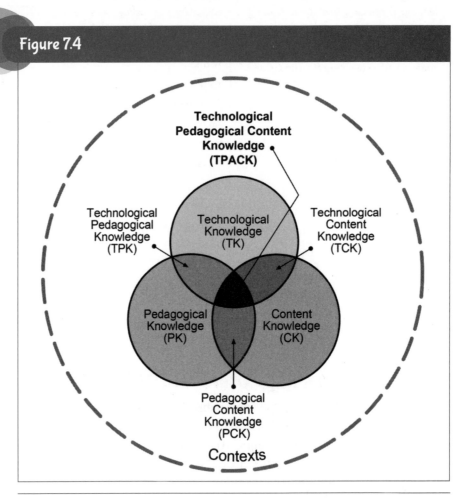

While at first glance this may looked pretty complex and scary and, really, who needs yet another tech integration model? But once you get past all the TLAs (Two Letter Acronyms), it's relatively simple, and can be used to thoughtfully evaluate software, apps, and educational websites.

Before using any technology resource with kids, complete a simple form based on the TPACK model.

Resource title: Digital photography	Example: Students will use a digital camera to record examples of living and nonliving objects in the school. These will be added to presentation slides organized by category.
CK: What is the content knowledge, skill set, or standard this resource will help you meet?	Students will understand the difference between living and nonliving objects and be able to identify them.
PK: What best-practice pedagogy does this resource use to help teach the content?	Increasing relevance by relating the learning to real-world objects in students' lives.
TK: What are the technical requirements of the resource? • Hardware and operating system • Internet availability • Age appropriateness • Secure and private • Complexity • Complete or trial version	Students will need access to a digital camera and a presentation program. This can be done at all grade levels with varying degrees of independence.

An important question that should be asked when selecting a technology tool is the demand it places on the student for original material. Does the program ask for original images, for example, or does it simply ask students to rearrange and use provided clip art-like elements?

Identifying the standard or pedagogy is why technology departments need to spend as much or more time with their counterparts in the teaching and learning departments as they do maintaining servers. It is a codependent relationship.

It's the Assignment, Not the Technology

So does using a program that generates a word cloud like the one that began this chapter encourage and allow creativity?

Did you guess it was a trick question?

While my word cloud itself doesn't demonstrate creative artistry, let's consider some other factors:

Was a standard template used? I used a precreated template of fonts and colors to create the graphic. Intrepid students can dig deeper and modify the design but not create their own fonts or cloud styles. If the text being used comes from a mystery story or historical essay, might the cloud be more effective if certain colors or fonts are chosen?

How original was the text that was used to make the cloud? Was it the student's own writing or text selected from another source?

Even programs and websites that allow students to "create" often stifle true originality through the clip art and templates that students are encouraged or required to use. This results in activity that is similar to coloring in a coloring book rather than drawing freehand, or building a Lego model from the instructions rather than building an original model through experimentation.

Look for programs that are containers in which students can place, edit, and display their own work. Animoto allows the use of self-taken photographs, blogs ask for original writing, and GarageBand allows experimentation of new musical composition. Simply rearranging a provided clip is not an especially creative act.

What was the purpose of the activity? If the goal of the assignment was to have students make an original graphic, better tools could have been used. If the reason for the assignment was to do an analysis of a writing's message by determining how many times certain words were used (a good way to analyze a political speech), then this is good start to developing, perhaps, an original means of interpretation.

Creativity will result in the assignment given, not the tools used. The expectation of creativity of some form is the only guarantee students will innovate. Don't let the professional look of the end product disguise a lack of original thinking or effectiveness.

Up for Discussion

1. Does technology that allows users to create expert-looking products without needing to learn traditional tools (think CAD/CAM vs. the drafting board) make people more or less creative?

2. Do some technology applications automatically bring out the creativity in the user?

3. By simply looking at a picture—graphic, drawing, photo—can the viewer know if creativity has been displayed?

4. Is a camera or a keyboard a more desirable feature in a student device?

5. How should professional development plans for educators reflect technology as a tool to develop creativity?

6. Has technology impacted your personal creativity?

8

Not Everything That Counts Can Be Measured

Can—or Should—Teachers Assess Creativity?

Creativity is a 21st century currency, and the best way to make sure it happens is to give points for it. They'll get with the program stat.

—Terry Heick (2013)

Based on interviews of over 5,000 adults in the United States, the United Kingdom, Germany, France, and Japan, the study "Creativity and Education: Why It Matters" (Adobe Systems, 2012) contains some interesting tidbits:

  78 percent of survey respondents believe creativity is important to their current career

  88 percent believe creativity should be built into education curriculum

94 percent agreed with the statement "It is important for educators to encourage creative thinking in their students."

But here are the scary findings:

80 percent of education majors (vs. 54 percent of engineering majors) believe "creativity is a skill you are born with"

47 percent of education majors felt there is enough opportunity in school for students to demonstrate creativity

41 percent of education majors felt academic test scores are the best indicators for success in school and beyond

Why the disconnect? Why does the general population believe creativity should be built into the education curriculum when education majors believe creativity is a genetic trait? Do 94 percent of practicing teachers encourage creative thinking in their students?

Might it be because we as educators are uncomfortable asking students to demonstrate something that we cannot *objectively* measure? (Remember Ms. Najran's difficulties in Chapter 2?) I have a lot of fun conducting workshops about creativity but one area that the workshops address makes me feel inadequate, and that's assessment.

Even if we ask for creativity, how do we know we've gotten it? Defining *creativity* is certainly a part of the solution—that not only should one recognize originality, but also the degree to which that originality improves the outcome through craftsmanship as we looked at in Chapter 2. But once we have a definition, what do we do with it? Craftsmanship and effectiveness have long been measured by educators. Originality? Not so much.

What would a test, rubric, checklist, narrative, or formative assessment look like that helps determine whether creativity was actually demonstrated—and at what level?

First, a word of caution. Assessment guru Grant Wiggins (2013a) warns that *poor* assessments can work against innovative thinking.

BAD rubrics kill creativity because they demand formulaic response. Good rubrics demand great results, and give students the freedom to cause them. Bottom line: if you signal in your rubrics that a powerful result is the goal you FREE up creativity and initiative. If you mandate format, content, and process and ignore the impact, you inhibit creativity and reward safe uncreative work.

Do we need to "measure" creativity or simply accept it as something that can't be measured? Can creativity and impact be measured separately?

Why Measure Creativity—or at Least Try?

- If you can't measure it, can you demonstrate it can be learned?
- If you can't measure it, can it be objectively and consistently scored?
- If you can't measure it, can you hold teachers accountable for teaching it?
- If you can't measure it, can it really be important?

Creativity is important enough that we give should pay attention to it when we assess students. No question.

I see two distinct ways of doing this: as a separate quality measured independently or as part of the total assessment of a total work.

Assessing Creativity by Itself

Ric Nudell, from Barre (VT) Technical Center, in reaction to one of my blog posts that asked if creativity was assessable, wrote

> As a Digital Media teacher I do try to help students develop creativity (or creative approaches to problem solving) so I do need to give them feedback on it, i.e. assess.
>
> This is one of the rubrics I use with students. It is a synthesis of a lot of research about the characteristics of creativity/creative approaches and forms a framework for conversations.

The tool on the next page is one of the most thoughtful attempts at measuring creativity I've seen. (And I would argue can be used to evaluate critical thinking as well.) When used, as Nudell suggests, it makes a powerful "framework for conversations." And conversation, as we remember from Chapter 3, is a valid type of formative assessment.

The Buck Institute for Education (BIE) website has a number of rubrics designed to assess creativity (Larmer, 2014). The BIE rubric has two parts: one to help evaluate the process and the other to help evaluate the product itself. It also had a "blank" fourth column that is labeled "Above Standard" because the authors

> realized that it's very hard to describe what creativity looks like when it goes beyond expectations. We found ourselves trying words like "wow factor" and "exceptionally" and "impressive" but they were just too vague and subjective. We decided it's a case of "you know it when you see it," so if a teacher and/or students want to write their own descriptors based on observations of extra-creative work, go for it!

Evidence of Creative Problem Solving Rubric

Project:

Student:

Category	Indicators of Evidence
Generating Ideas	• Fluency: generated many ideas • Flexibility: looked at problem in a variety of ways • Originality: ideas are different than what is already out there • Elaboration: adding nuance, making ideas richer • Symbolic thinking: making connections, comparisons, analogies
Digging Deeper Into Ideas	• Analyzing: thinking about what makes the idea(s) work • Synthesizing: putting one or more ideas together • Reorganizing/redefining: modifying the original ideas • Resolving ambiguity: clarifying, focusing, refining ideas • Working with complexity: building relationships, levels
Openness and Courage to Explore Ideas	• Problem sensitivity: matching solutions to initial problems • Curiosity and risk taking: out-of-the-box ideas • Humor, playfulness, fantasy, feelings: inner emotional content • Integration of dichotomies: inclusion of opposing concepts • Growth: working with ideas/places that are personally new
Listening to One's Inner Voice	• Sense of purpose: reasons for choices • Persistence/hard work: followed vision to completion • Rejection of stereotypes: concepts move beyond stereotypes

Student: _____ (date)   Peer: _____ (date)   Instructor: _____ (date)

Assessment: Excellent   Good   Fair   Poor

Source: R. Nudell, 2014.

In classes like art or design, creative writing, or business entrepreneurship, in which one of the stated objectives is some form of innovative thinking, a tool like the one above may be needed as a form of summative assessment.

Assessing Creativity as a Part of the Evaluation

Do we really want to evaluate creativity in and of itself—or do we want to evaluate the impact creativity may have on the effectiveness of a product, a solution, or a task as Wiggins suggests above?

Let's look at a little bit less sophisticated but still effective assessment tool. This short checklist is designed to be used for a cross-disciplinary project in science, math, and information/technology literacy. Elementary students are asked to pick a "favorite city" and over the course of three weeks apply what they have learned about graphing to create one that shows the high temperatures for each day.

Temperature Graph for Climate in:	
My Online Source of Information:	
___ Yes ___ No ___ ?	1. My graph has a title.
___ Yes ___ No ___ ?	2. My grid is set up correctly.
___ Yes ___ No ___ ?	3. The numbers are easy to read and evenly spaced.
___ Yes ___ No ___ ?	4. Points are plotted correctly on the grid.
___ Yes ___ No ___ ?	5. Temperatures are written correctly.
___ Yes ___ No ___ ?	6. Lines are straight and connect the points.
___ Yes ___ No ___ ?	7. I have plotted three full weeks of temperatures.
___ Yes ___ No ___ ?	8. I have used my own artwork to illustrate something people living in my city might be doing because of these temperatures.

As Heick in the chapter's purposely ironic opening quote suggests, simply "add a column for 'Creativity' on every rubric" and you can fake having a 21st century classroom. But if you've read this far in the book, you are not interested in simply giving the appearance of being a progressive, caring educator.

What Heick's comment does suggest is that there may be at least a couple reasons why teachers might add a column for creativity to authentic assessment tools. If showing creativity simply adds to the point total of a summative assessment, we've suddenly gone from an intrinsic to extrinsic motivation model. Let's assume that most of your efforts to assess creativity will be formative rather than summative in nature. Go right ahead and add that column without the least bit of guilt.

Educator Shawn McCusker (2013) warns that "placing a list of 'have to's' at the top of a rubric is like building a wall at the bottom of a slide. It completely destroys the ride and subverts the joy of the creative process, providing an off-switch." He advises eliminating checklists that define "exemplary," avoid having too many rules or limits in the rubric, and use language that encourages risk taking—words like "daring" and "unique."

The Subjectivity Paradox

As students get older and our expectations of them grow, we may need to discriminate among varying degrees of creativity. A "simple yes, no or ?" doesn't seem to suffice.

Assessment guru Susan Brookhart (2013) writes that rubrics can help clarify criteria for success and show "what the continuum of performance looks like, from low to high, from imitative to very creative." She offers a rubric for creativity that ranges from "**Very Creative:** Ideas represent a startling variety of important concepts from different contexts or disciplines" to "**Ordinary/Routine:** Ideas represent important concepts from the same or similar contexts or disciplines," and adds a final ranking, "**Imitative**," for evaluating the variety of ideas and contexts shown in a work.

One of the genuine deficiencies of many rubrics is the ambiguous nature of the terms. Note the terms *startling*, *important*, and *same*. Other indicators in the rubric include the terms *wide variety*, *original and surprising*, *interesting*, and *helpful*. What separates *excellent* and *good*? These are all qualifiers of student work that are highly subjective. What is *original* or *startling* to a first-grader may be tired old stuff to his teacher—and perhaps vice versa.

One way of overcoming the inherently subjective nature of scoring the degree to which a student product or idea is effective or original is to use multiple assessors. We've discussed how project rubrics and checklists need to be given to students at the beginning of the assignment; we haven't examined who should actually complete them and when.

My suggestion is to use assessment tools on a regular basis on longer projects. Each week, after each subtask is completed, or after every draft, students can check to see what's complete, what's in progress, and what's yet needed. This way these tools become true tools for improvement over time.

In Chapter 5, I suggested that projects that allow creativity have results that are shared with people who care and respond. Note that Nudell's rubric above includes blanks for the student, a peer, and the instructor to each rate the project. If the assignment is team based, each member should rate each element that is being assessed. Comparing and discussing multiple results may reduce inaccuracy or unfairness in an inherently subjective evaluation. Figure skating in the Olympics, among other events, uses multiple judges for just that reason.

I would also add parents and guardians as potential assessors. While no one wants parents doing the child's work for them, I believe we can define a role for them. When my less-than-enthusiastic-about-school son came home from a science class with a mousetrap and the assignment that it needed to power a self-made car, he descended into his basement lair. After a very short time, I heard the familiar soundtrack of a videogame coming up the stairs. When I asked him to show me his product, the duct-taped set of K'NEX plastic parts leapt six inches in the air before crashing to the floor. I suggest to him the assignment was to build a vehicle that moves horizontally, not a helicopter, and that he could play videogames after his project could move at least five feet across the floor. "Quality control" is the correct role for parents and they can help provide that if they too have the assignment and instrument with which the product will be judged. All teachers should have links to project assignments and assessments on their classroom websites for easy parental access.

Older students, local experts, public blog comments, and students in classes in other schools can prove useful for any given assessment effort. Just use your imagination.

Forgive me a short rant. In our one-right-answer, test-driven educational environment, we somehow lost our faith in subjective evaluation. Yes, many projects that we as adults must complete have some form of metric. Did the project come in on time and under budget? Did the project have its intended effect? Did we sell more widgets as a result of the project? By meeting metrics like this, we can objectively show success or failure. But truly successful projects have less measurable outcomes as well. Did the team who completed the project work well together? Were there unintended consequences of the project? Has the company's reputation and public image improved as a result of the project? Subjective evaluations still have a place in organizational work—and especially in schools. One big difference between a teacher and computer program is that the teacher has a heart.

And as Einstein also famously observed, "Not everything that can be counted counts, and not everything that counts can be counted."

Self-Assessment

Knowing that creative and self-motivated people constantly evaluate the quality of their own work, I always asked students in graduate classes not to just complete projects but also to turn in a detailed self-assessment in the form of a rubric or checklist. What many found was that while creating a school library floor plan or a policy manual wasn't particularly difficult, creating a tool to effectively evaluate their final product was extremely challenging. In fact, they often reported spending more time of the checklist than they did on the actual task.

There is, of course, madness to the method of this approach. A good assessment asks the student to formally consider if all required elements of the task were completed. It should ask why their approach was the best one. And it can and should ask if the thinking that went into the effort was their own—not just a regurgitation of other ideas.

As a smaller percentage of our workers are employees and more workers are self-employed, this ability to self-evaluate becomes critical. The engineer, the plumber, the salesperson, and the technology entrepreneur don't have bosses standing over their shoulders evaluating their tasks. Those who see themselves as risk-taking entrepreneurs need good metrics to show their innovative efforts have had the desired result.

A Fool's Errand?

Are we on a fool's errand in looking at ways to assess creativity? Does teaching true creativity require second-order, not first-order, change in how we measure student learning? Evaluating originality within traditional assessment methods may not work.

Educators will need to stop looking at student work as right or wrong, but perhaps as effective or ineffective. A student must still show mastery of disciplinary knowledge and craftsmanship, but with originality being a critical component. So questions will come up like

- Did your new approach to solving this math problem result in an accurate answer?

- Did your original poem elicit the emotional response you intended?

- Did your trial use of plastic wheels give your vehicle better mileage?

- Did your experimental free-throw style result in increased shots made?

- Did your "crazy" campaign result in less trash in the school hallways?

Perhaps results are the true measure of creativity and innovation. Did your new approach work and why or why not?

The creative iPhone wasn't just a device that was more aesthetically appealing. The true innovation was that the device became a small, external brain that made people themselves more effective.

Up for Discussion

1. Does subjectivity play a role in evaluating student work? Are we demeaning educators when we dismiss their ability to make judgments that can't be quantified?

2. Is creativity better assessed independently or as portion of a total evaluation instrument? Are there situations in which each type of assessment might work better? Which may result in greater amounts of originality?

3. Should all assessment address the degree of innovation shown?

4. How important is a person's ability to self-assess the quality of his or her own work? How do we help students develop this disposition?

5. Can you identify the "wow factor" in a student's work when you see it? What makes it "wow"?

Chapter 9

I Stole the Idea From the Internet

How Can Educators Become More Professionally Creative?

> When people are doing work that they love and they're allowed to deeply engage in it—and when the work itself is valued and recognized—then creativity will flourish. Even in tough times.
>
> —Teresa Amabile (quoted in Breen, 2004)

A memorable piece of advice I received as a student teacher was that one's students may not learn from what we say, but they always learn from what we do. It is not enough to preach our values as educators; we must model them as well. Does this also hold true for creativity? If we want our kids to be creative, must we also demonstrate it?

In order to answer that question, we need to tackle some other questions first: Is creativity demonstrated by teachers in and of itself a prima facie good? Do we as educators have the potential of doing as much harm with new approaches as we have of helping students? Should we treat experimenting with a child's intellectual health any differently than we treat experimenting with a child's physical health?

When academic researchers want to use human subjects in their experiments, a great deal of paperwork and permission gathering is required. When the procedure or process is risky enough, we try the experiment on laboratory animals first—and not without heartfelt concern by many.

Yet I am going to encourage you as a classroom teacher to experiment on small children. Every day.

Until *every* child is working to her fullest capacity and ability, teachers should be devising and trying new approaches to learning in their classrooms. For children who are not engaged, who are not successful when we use standard practices and materials, or who display behaviors that keep themselves and their classmates from learning, we have an ethical obligation to use different methods with them.

If teachers expect children to be creative, they need to model creative approaches to their own practice as well. And it may be that empathy for original thinkers is only possible by those who are themselves innovative.

Educators who wish to deviate from research-based best practices, established curricula, and adopted resources (and wish to use either technology or leeches), the following requirements ought to be in place:

1. The purpose of the changed practice needs to be clearly stated in terms of a student outcome.

2. There needs to be a quantifiable method of measuring the effect of the new practice.

3. The result of the experiment/creative approach is shared with other professionals in such manner that it can be replicated.

4. The rigor of the above requirements is high, all experiments be externally monitored, and all data be statistically validated when possible.

Would we ask any less of those whom we entrust our kids' physical health? Remember our definition of creativity from Chapter 2—that creativity shows originality, effectiveness, and craftsmanship. In this case, best teaching practices are the craftsmanship element (see Figure 9.1).

One of the reasons that we have a dependence on norm-based, high-stakes testing is that the educational establishment itself has never addressed its own accountability to the satisfaction of the public. Now we are chafing under these short-sighted (but measurable) metrics non-educators have

Figure 9.1

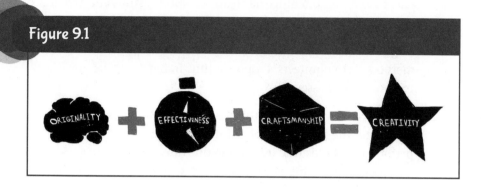

placed on our shoulders. If we are to be creative in our methodology, to use new technology tools, to emphasize new skills over basic skills, it's imperative we make accountability a part of our efforts—and respect parents', employers', and the public's need for it. Do we really want to continue to be known as good-hearted, but fuzzy-headed, *artistes*?

How Can Educators Take Creative Professional Risks?

So as educators, especially classroom teachers, how do we get our creative ideas accepted when, as we'll examine more fully in the next chapter, many people, often one's own supervisor, are naturally inclined to stay wedged securely in their own boxes of tradition?

1. **Call it *innovative* rather than *creative*.** While generally these terms can be used interchangeably, there are nuances in their definitions. To innovate has the connotation of making changes in something already established. To create has the more extreme connotation of bringing something completely new (and scary) into existence. Vygotsky's proximal theory says to learn something new we have to have a connection with the known. Can your creative idea be implemented in baby steps—extending an established practice rather than inventing a whole new practice?

2. **Make your change-resistant supervisor think it is his idea.** Try starting a conversation about a proposed innovation with "I think you were mentioning the other day about changing the process we use to _____. Have you given this anymore thought? I personally think it's a good idea and here's a way we might tweak it. . . ." No such strategy is needed for administrators who encourage new ways of solving old problems, of course.

3. **Stress the functionality, not the newness.** Too often we forget the second third of what makes something creative—that it is

effective. When pitching the creative solution, stress effectiveness of the solution, not the originality of the idea.

4. **Suggest a trial run and evaluation.** Run a pilot test of the new method. Get volunteers. Propose a time frame. Describe how the method will be assessed.

5. **Build trusting relationships and a track record.** The old adage that the best predictor of future performance is past performance holds true in leading innovative and creative approaches to solving problems. When suggesting your idea, it wouldn't hurt to mention how your similar approaches to problem solving worked before. And if you don't have a track record of success? Well, maybe people ought to be nervous about your ideas and running your ideas by others is advisable.

6. **Seek recognition.** Many leaders like recognition for their programs, schools, or districts. If an innovative program might lead to a state or national award, use that to sell it. This seems the least genuine reason to do anything creative. I'd hope most of us in education try new things for the sake of improving kids' educational experiences, not for personal glory.

7. **Be subversive.** Just do it. Ask forgiveness later if needed.

It's tough selling an original idea when it means upsetting somebody's routine. But using strategic and creative thinking, it can be done.

Learning From a PLN

As we examined earlier, creativity often loves company. We tend to be more creative when we surround ourselves with others who like to try new things as well. Happily, even teachers working in schools where they may feel they are the only innovative person on staff can still surround themselves with others like them. They just need to do it virtually.

The term *personal learning network* (PLN) has been a part of technology junkies' vocabulary for many years, and the tools and skills needed to take advantage of networked learning continue to evolve. I define a PLN as a self-created set of experts, colleagues, and resources that can be relied upon to meet daily learning needs, usually dependent on networked technology. I got my first taste of a PLN in the early 1990s when an e-mail list of school librarians from around the country—and later around the world—got started. That e-mail list provided me, as the only librarian in my school, a simple, online opportunity for sharing resources, asking questions, venting, and trumpeting successes with others.

Prior to the Internet, continuing education for teachers and administrators consisted of reading professional journals, attending conferences, and taking college classes all seasoned with a soupçon of local inservice. Each of these resources is still available and important. But given the pace and degree of change in schools, traditional education methods alone have been insufficient to keep most thoughtful educators current.

However, many educators have built PLNs using networked technologies and become accustomed to learning on a daily basis—at times most convenient to them. They regularly read, listen, respond, and argue with the wisdom and viewpoints ranging from those of vaunted academics at world-class universities to the classroom teacher down the hall, from international futurists and visionaries to those who share their own positions in districts similar to their own. These connected educators have become a part of a tribe that encourages, sympathizes, and supports members who are willing to take the risks necessary to do things differently.

Educators should be well past the experimental stage of using PLNs and settling into a more mature, more thoughtful use of time spent engaged in our daily learning. It's imperative one's PLN use evolves. The noise-to-value ratio remains high with digital communication, while job-related time commitments of teachers continue to grow. Therefore, accurate discrimination among information and opinion sources is a professional skill that's increasingly important. Happily, the technology tools for creating a PLN are also evolving, helping *personal* become the operative word in personal learning network.

While mailing lists and electronic newsletters are still valuable methods of keeping up and keeping in touch with current educational issues and forming communities of practice, many connected educators are also finding value in

1. **Social networks.** Most of us are familiar with the giant Web 2.0 "networks" Facebook, Google+, and LinkedIn. If these seem overwhelming, try a more profession-specific or local network. Larger organizations often provide members with their own pages and allow smaller special interests groups to form within the larger network. (Think SIGs—special interest groups within the ISTE organization for librarians, teacher educators, administrators, and computer teachers, among others.) They are aimed at creating real-people connections among professionals with like interests and challenges.

2. **Content aggregators.** Blogs and podcasts let educators read or hear, react, and converse on the latest thinking by educational leaders. Information on blogs tends to be timely, short, and often

opinionated. If you have a favorite blogger, examine her blogrolls for leads to related bloggers worth reading. The quickest strategy to manage your reading and keep up with those blogs you enjoy is to subscribe to their RSS feeds and group them in one Web page through an aggregator or reader like Feedly or Netvibes.

3. **Virtual meetings and presentations.** Webcasts, presentations, and workshops done via Internet tools like GoToMeeting or Elluminate eliminate windshield time and costs. Webinars, attended at our desks, allow us to get inspiration from keynotes without paying airfare or conference registration. Watch your e-mail for "web seminars" and check conference websites to see what sessions might be streamed or archived. Informal video meetings using Google+ Hangouts or Skype are increasingly common among schools.

4. **Repositories of high-quality educational resources.** TED Talks and other online presentations can delight, inform, and motivate. Some of the best minds in the world share their ideas in free lectures. Universities like Brown and Massachusetts Institute of Technology have placed their best courses online for free viewing. Expand your horizons and make creative connections by taking a class, say, on archaeology. Maybe you will understand some of your older faculty members a little better.

5. **Twitter.** Microblogging allows users to follow other professionals "tweets"—short posts of 140 or fewer characters. The real trick for success in Twitter is finding the right folks to follow. Those experts whose articles you read, whose conference sessions you attend, and whose classes you have taken are likely Tweeters. Start with them. You'll find that Tweeters will share their exceptional blog posts, their favorite web-based tools, and publications they find of value. I guarantee that you'll find at least one great idea every day. If you have a particular area of interest, search Twitter by hashtags—#creativity for example.

6. **MOOCs.** Taking a massive open online course (MOOC) is a free and flexible way of learning about a new topic. While the recorded lectures by often notable experts and quality readings may form the core of the course, making connections through online discussions with other professionals taking the course may prove to be the most valuable component of a MOOC for many people.

You will not have to look long or hard to find others online who are willing to support your creative ideas through social media. When the going gets tough, the tough get in touch with their colleagues.

Communities and Competitions
Dedicated to Creativity

You are not alone. The promulgation of creativity is important to enough people that many are doing something about it. These established organizations and efforts reduce the isolation teachers too often feel when working on creative activities with students:

1. **Center for Creative Learning** (www.creativelearning.com) is a consulting organization with a strong research base. Led by Dr. Don Treffinger, the center primarily offers paid services but does have a newsletter, *Creative Learning Today*, and many other free resources.

2. **Consortium for Entrepreneurship Education** (www.entre-ed .org) primarily supports business educators, sponsoring an annual National Entrepreneurship Week and a national conference.

3. **Destination Imagination** (www.destinationimagination.org) is a venerable nonprofit organization that focuses on global projects, the most popular being the Our Challenge competition.

4. **Google Science Fair** (www.googlesciencefair.com/en) is an annual online competition that asks students to identify what they love, what they are good at, and how they want to change the world.

5. **Spark!Lab Invent It Challenge** (challenges.epals.com), cosponsored by the Smithsonian and ePals, allows both individuals and groups to compete in four age categories in devising solutions to real-world problems.

6. **Odyssey of the Mind** (www.odysseyofthemind.com) is among the largest and oldest programs in which international teams solve problems in a wide number of categories for students ranging in educational levels from kindergarten to college.

7. **Tournament of Minds** (www.tom.edu.au) is a problem-solving contest for students in Australia, New Zealand, and Southeast Asia.

8. **Makerspace** (makerspace.com) provides a directory of community makerspaces as well as a blog dealing with creating and using these resources.

9. **School-Wide Innovation Day** (blog.cue.org/school-wide-innovation -day), sponsored by CUE (Computer-Using Educators), is a grassroots effort to give students an entire day of "ownership and choice."

10. **FIRST LEGO League Team** (www.firstlegoleague.org) has over 20,000 teams in over 70 countries that ask students to program robots, develop effective teams, develop innovative solutions to a global problem, and present their solutions in creative ways.

Stanford professor David Kelley (Kelley & Kelley, 2012) suggests that an educator's job is not to teach creativity but to help students "rediscover their creative confidence—the natural ability to come up with new ideas and the courage to try them out." Many of us as educators need to rediscover our own creative confidence as well. And we can do it through collegiality, through practice, and through courage.

Up for Discussion

1. Under what circumstances does a teacher have a professional obligation to be creative? Are there circumstances in which being a creative practitioner may be inappropriate or harmful?

2. The de-professionalization of teaching is a major concern of many educators. What causes this and how might creativity play a role in reversing this trend?

3. What might a schoolwide attempt to foster creativity among all students look like?

4. What factors make your professional learning network useful?

Change Is Good . . . You Go First

Why Do We Love Creativity but Fear Creative People?

*I can't understand why people are frightened of new ideas.
I'm frightened of the old ones.*

—John Cage

Developing creativity in the classroom, in the school, or in the district is not particularly difficult. As we've examined in previous chapters, simple teaching techniques can spur divergent thinking. Innovation can be a part of all content areas and disciplines. Any project can have recognition of originality in its assessment. But creativity is too often actively suppressed by teachers and administrators. Here's why.

Creativity means doing something differently, looking at the world in a new way, potentially changing existing power structures. Any wonder human nature is a little suspicious of "creative types"? One of our Neanderthal ancestors may well have reasoned, "Gee, we had a 17.5 percent success rate of killing mammoths using the atal method. This new-fangled bow and arrow might be worse! And what do will we do about Mr. Phlegm who is headman because of his atal chucking prowess?" (see Figure 10.1).

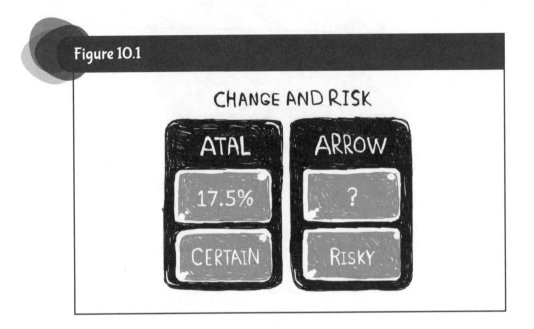

Figure 10.1

Many of us in education actually fear creativity—whether we like to admit it or not, whether we're conscious of it or not.

Chomsky and the Purpose of School—and Other Reasons We as Educators Are Afraid of Creativity

There are a number of reasons we are creativity averse in schools, and we need to recognize those reasons before we can overcome them.

1. **Creativity upsets the organizational status quo.** Creative approaches to education mean change. And change always means there are winners and losers—in power, in budgets, in comfort levels. Even if one has been only modestly successful in one's role at school, with change it *could* get worse. Any truly creative approach to solving a problem runs a real risk of causing harm instead of resulting in improvement. Educators don't like risk—not because we are cowards—but because our task of helping children to be successful is too important to take unnecessary chances. Morally, many of us feel that innovation should be the last arrow in our quiver of tools, not the first one for which we reach.

2. **Creativity runs counter to the traditional mission society has given school—to create conformists.** Linguist Noam Chomsky (Falcone, 2013) observes that mass public education in the late 19th century was designed to turn "independent farmers, many of them pretty radical" into "tools for someone else" as factory workers. Chomsky shares Ralph Waldo Emerson's view that mass public education helps keep citizens in line by training them in obedience and servility "so they're not going to think through the way the world works and come after [political leaders'] throats." The argument can still easily be made that society's charge to education is to maintain social order—certainly not to foment revolution.

3. **Creativity changes relationships.** Hugh MacLeod accurately reports that "a big idea will change you" (MacLeod, 2009). We may like or dislike any individual student, but at least we know them and how to deal with them. Creative students grow in unpredictable ways. Creative people can be just plain uncomfortable to be around. And we as educators love our "norms."

   In fact, when teachers "were asked to rate their students on a variety of personality measures—the list included everything from 'individualistic' to 'risk-seeking' to 'accepting of authority'—the traits most closely aligned with creative thinking were also closely associated with their 'least favorite' students" (Westby & Dawson, 1995). Other studies have shown that highly creative students will avoid and even subvert traditional educational work if the work is not seen as related to their personal interests (Sparks, 2011).

4. **Creativity offends sensibilities.** Artists (visual, musical, etc.) have always had the ability to shock. I'll bet that the Cro-Magnon (probably a teenager) who used two sticks to beat on a hollow log instead of just one was driven from the cave. My dad couldn't stand rock and roll and bell-bottom jeans, and I find today's rap music and sagging trousers fashions tough to appreciate. Language or visuals one's own generation may find obscene or distasteful are often perfectly acceptable by kids—like it or not.

5. **Creativity upsets the experts.** The more specialized a person is in a field, the more fixed the mindset (Michalko, 2011). Do not expect enthusiasm from those whose identity, expertise, and livelihood are challenged by an innovation. We see this in the technology world often—resistance from technicians who maintain local servers when organizations move storage and application to the Internet cloud; when professional photographers cling to film cameras and chemical developing rather than shift to digital cameras

and editing; or when we as teachers keep a firm grip on our textbooks when computer tablets offer access to resources that are more current, more relevant, and more easily individualized.

6. **Creativity makes us feel inferior and puts us on a learning curve.** When the tech department asks us to use a creative means of using a tool, we may feel inadequate since we may not have the skills necessary to use the tool itself well. Teachers may feel intimidated by students who have greater familiar with technology. (The cure for this is to consider oneself a colearner, not just teacher.) As parents ask to be contacted using social media, our learning curve's grade rises again. Ask a person to do something new usually means time spent learning and practicing new skills—and sometimes failing. Why does *your* being creative always seem to mean more work for *me*?

7. **Creativity isn't always fun.** Teacher John Spencer (2014) reminds us that nearly all creative acts contain elements of tedium, frustration, and anxiety and asks "how do we create structures and policies that encourage students to work creatively even when things get tough, boring or confusing?" In giving students opportunities to practice the dispositions that fan the spark of creativity that we examined in Chapter 2, including grit and risk tolerance, are we as educators prepared for students who are not happy learners who demand immediate successes?

8. **Creativity undermines our efforts to create good test takers.** The antithesis of creativity is asking for the "one right answer" which is exactly what happens when educators ask students to regurgitate on standardized tests. (Ever wonder why they were called *standardized*?) Tests are timed; creativity takes time. Tests are supposedly objective; creativity is often subjective. Tests demand respect for the authority of the test takers; creativity questions and often defies authority. And when one's professional evaluation and even salary may depend on one's students filling in the "correct" bubble, creativity becomes an enemy.

9. **Creativity is hard to measure or categorize.** Which is more creative? A new vocal interpretation of a classic song or a new computer program that helps a diabetic monitor his blood sugar? The song will be assessed by music critics—and by the music-purchasing public. The software will be judged by a single factor—it works reliably or it doesn't. You can't place students or their ideas on a creativity bell curve. There are no creativity Lexiles. Teachers especially have been led to doubt the value of their subjective judgments about their students.

10. **Creativity may mean we adults are expected to demonstrate creativity as well.** School cultures that value creativity ask for it from students *and* staff. But I am doing everything perfectly now. Why change?

The first step for putting creativity back into the classroom may very well be our personal acknowledgment that creativity scares us as individuals. There may not be a full twelve steps to being a recovering creative-averse educator, but recognition that creativity can be frightening is a good first tiptoe.

Accepting the Challenge of Truly Creative Students and Peers

So are there antidotes to creativity aversion? Here are some things that work for me—sometimes.

I try to remember that students grow and improve through creative approaches to problems and that they are practicing real-world dispositions. Any particular stage of growth may be uncomfortable for us as adults, but no one is really ever a finished product. If we truly honor our own creativity, we must recognize that we ourselves may make others uncomfortable—our peers, our supervisors, and even our students. But in honoring our creativity, we also are acknowledging that the final product of our innovation will be an improved circumstance. The bumpy road may well lead to a beautiful destination.

Rather than fight or ignore student creativity, as professionals, we need to use that power. Those students who challenge the system, if given a task or problem to solve, can harness the energy for positive results. Have you asked that off-topic kid to figure out how he would keep the class on track?

I think of how much of a geezer I sound like when I start a sentence with "I can't believe today's kids' tastes in _____." And I try to remember what my parents hated about the way I dressed, what I listened to, and how I wore my hair. (But you probably really shouldn't have gotten that tattoo.)

Everyone needs to remember that creativity demands craftsmanship. Content knowledge, good skills, and other testable kinds of stuff are not antithetical to creativity—but critical. Think assessment balance—although I know our politicians make this tough. Creativity is taking craftsmanship to a higher level, not replacing it.

We should reexamine the value of subjectivity when we deal with kids and their accomplishments. We are forcing way too many "round" kids into very "square" holes. Think personalization of education—evaluating each person's accomplishments personally, as well as their using their interests as a guide to their education. And remember to ask not if a child is creative, but how that child is creative.

Finally, if you don't want to try new things, take some risks, be adventurous, have a divergent (even subversive) thought now and then, think about finding a new line of work since you've lost your passion for education and are perhaps just collecting the paycheck.

Does Your School Culture Embrace Creativity—or Stifle It?

Business is very interested in how to make employees more creative. Teresa Amabile at the Harvard Business School conducted a study that reviewed 12,000 daily journal entries from 238 people working on creative projects in seven companies. She discovered some interesting myths companies need to recognize if they want to increase creativity in their employees (Breen, 2004).

What I find interesting is that these business myths have direct correlations to education if we stretch our thinking even a little.

> **Myth 1: Creativity comes from creative types**. Anyone with normal intelligence who is intrinsically motivated can show creativity. School application: We need to recognize that all students, not just those in the talented and gifted programs, AP classes, or on a college track, have the capacity to be innovative, especially when intrinsically motivated.

> **Myth 2: Money is a creativity motivator.** When people believe their pay is dependent on performance, they become risk averse—and less likely to be creative. School application: Grades, class rank, or even winning competitions are not the key to making students more creative. The truly original thinkers work out of personal need and interest, not for high test scores. In fact, worrying about grades and other extrinsic motivators will also make students risk averse and less likely to take creative chances.

> **Myth 3: Time pressure fuels creativity.** When working under pressure, people's creativity declines—and stays reduced—because they can't deeply engage with the problem. School application: Fifty-minute classes, overstuffed curricula, and too much deadline-driven homework will kill creativity in kids. How many kids get time in school (or life) to reflect and dream—or are even encouraged to do so?

> **Myth 4: Fear forces breakthroughs.** People are more likely to have an innovative breakthrough if they were happy the day before, so one day's happiness can predict the next day's creativity. School application: Our children's overall attitude toward school is a critical factor in helping them exercise their creative muscles. Kids who don't like school,

feel isolated or depressed, or are always under pressure will not become original problem solvers.

Myth 5: Competition beats collaboration. People stop sharing ideas and groups become less creative when they compete instead of collaborate, having the confidence to share and debate ideas. School application: Creativity needs to be recognized through means other than competitions. Ranking and awards may discourage the entrepreneurial spirit. Grades are less effective than performance assessments in bringing out the creativity energies of kids.

Myth 6: A streamlined organization is a creative organization. When businesses downsize, people's anxiety cause them to disengage from their work. School application: Huge class sizes, inadequate beleaguered staff, crumbling facilities, and disappearing extracurricular opportunities are the equivalent of business downsizing. Reducing school budgets may well reduce the number of creative graduates as well.

Business and education are two very different animals. But human nature is human nature whether that human is a senior-level accountant or a third-grade student. When no-nonsense business experts recognize the factors that encourage or inhibit creativity, all of us ought to pay attention.

So does your school's culture inhibit or encourage creativity in its students and employees? Often formed over dozens of years, the values, habits, and climates of school buildings are incredibly difficult to change. Culture outlasts teachers and administrators, lean and rich budget years, and a vast array of new programs, theories, and strategic plans.

I would never discourage anyone from attempting to change a school culture—especially one that is having a negative impact on students. But sane people also look for employment and services in places where a positive culture already exists. Were I looking for a school in which to work or in which to enroll my children, I'd be looking for some of these attributes:

1. **School climate.** Funny how a person can sense the safety, friendliness, and sense of caring within minutes of walking into a school. Little things like cleanliness, open doors to classrooms, laughter, respectful talk, presence of volunteers, and genuine smiles from both adults and kids are the barometers of school climate. Creativity flourishes in schools that care about their students and staff.

2. **Student work is honored.** The hallways, display cases, and teacher bulletin boards should all be used to show and recognize products and accomplishments of the students currently enrolled in the school. Yes, it's OK to have a wall of famed alumni or old sports trophies, but make sure today's kids get a chance to share their

original work and ideas publicly as well. This also goes for the virtual hallways of the school website.

3. **Public contests and fairs.** Science fairs, history days, math competitions, knowledge bowls, speech contests, inventors' competitions, and a host of other possibilities should play a role in students' educational experiences at all grade levels. A public display of creativity and innovation gives students the opportunity to display the courage needed to be a change agent.

4. **Arts for all in the elementary school.** In our mad rush to ensure all students are capable of demonstrating the one-right-answer mentality on standardized tests, elementary schools have misguidedly cut regular art, music, and physical education opportunities to obtain more time for direct reading and math instruction. Schools that maintain arts offerings for all students maintain the chances for all students to demonstrate creativity.

5. **Elective and extracurricular offerings.** What happens in class is important. But so is what happens during the other 140 hours of the week. Elementary schools need to offer after-school clubs and activities that develop social skills and interests. Secondary schools must be rich with art, sports, technology education, music, and community service choices that develop individual talents, leadership, pride in accomplishment, and pragmatic innovative problem-solving abilities.

6. **Good libraries.** The quality of the library is the clearest sign of how much a school values reading, teaching for independent thinking, personalizing education, and lifelong learning. A trained librarian and a welcoming environment with a well-used collection of current physical books and magazines—along with e-resources and minimally filtered Internet access—tell a parent that the teachers and principal value more than the memorization of facts from a textbook, that a diversity of ideas and opinions is important, and that reading is not just necessary, but pleasurable and important. And that creativity is valued both in production and appreciation.

7. **Open classrooms.** There are two facets to open classrooms. The first is the classroom with an open door, uncovered windows, and guests within—parents, volunteers, specialists. The second facet of the open classroom involves openness to new ideas and expressions—the kind of openness we discussed in Chapter 6. Lively discussions and open-ended genuine questions are the hallmarks of this openness.

8. **Project-based learning.** Demonstrating competencies through projects and performance is the primary opportunity that students have to practice all three elements of creativity: originality,

effectiveness, and craftsmanship. When authentically evaluated using a formative assessment strategy, student creativity grows.

9. **Technology used to create, not just consume.** Aligned to this project-based model is how technologies are being used in the classroom. Is that school tablet just an e-book, video monitor, and game console—or is it used to produce original graphics, podcasts, videos, writings, and other communications?

10. **Commitment to professional development.** The amount of exciting research on effective teaching practices and schools is overwhelming. Brain-based research, reflective practice, systematic examination of student work, strategies for working with disengaged students, and the effective use of technology are some of the findings that can have a positive impact on how to best teach children. But research doesn't do any good if it stays in the university or journal. Good schools give financial priority to teaching teachers how to improve their practice. These schools don't just call in the consultants, but honor the knowledge and professionalism of their teaching staff by finding means for teachers to work together in professional learning communities on a regular basis during work hours.

11. **Individual teacher quality.** Overall school ratings may be deceptive. Five-star teachers who promote creativity can be found in one-star schools, and one-star teachers who primarily teach to the test can be found in five-star schools. Parents may encounter either situation. I always listened to what other parents said about the teachers my children might have and insisted that my kids got the teachers with good reviews—to the dismay of many a school principal. If I had children in school today, I'd be visiting the very interesting Rate My Teacher website—the educational version of Angie's List.

12. **Genuine student governance.** Schools with positive cultures respect students, and no greater respect can be shown by giving students themselves a role in the governance of the school. Whether it's in the form of a student council that has real power, a student-selected and -directed school play, students serving on building committees, or teachers asking students to formulate classroom norms and rules, adults in schools give students real-world problem-solving abilities by giving them real-world problems. And trust.

13. **Understanding that play is essential.** Research shows that if we want more creative, innovative students we need to give them time to play. "Play gives children space to dream, discover, improvise, and challenge convention" (Townsend, 2014). In good schools you will find teachers who find ways to give students unstructured time and space to play—and I will bet you find happier children as well.

In Chapter 4, we examined the different ways students can demonstrate creativity. A school with a creativity-positive culture will not have a single great program but give students the chance to shine in many different ways—artistically, athletically, academically, and socially.

Whether we like it or not, in many states, school report cards based on a very limited test-driven data set are ratcheting up competition among schools. Schools with high test scores wave them like a banner to attract parent-consumers. But schools' self-evaluation (and public relations) efforts need to go beyond bragging about test-based data and need to include other quality criteria as well. Parents *do* understand that creativity, perhaps even more than calculus, is a critical ability.

Is the Common Core just one more war in this battle in turning independent Americans into believers instead of thinkers? I am genuinely saddened when reading about huge technology initiatives like those of the Los Angeles (CA) school district spending $30 million on iPads to "support the Common Core" instead of using them as tools for creativity. Technology in many places seems to be just one more nail in the coffin of conformity into which we are placing our students.

Yet at least one happier, more optimistic study has found that education as a whole is becoming more innovative. In a study over twenty-five countries published in 2014, the Organisation for Economic Co-operation and Development finds "there have been large increases in innovative pedagogic practices across all countries studied for this report in areas such as relating lessons to real life, higher order skills, data and text interpretation and personalisation of teaching" with the United States being among the top five with the greatest increases. Let's hope this trend of educators to employ new educational practices that will lead to more attention to creativity continues.

Will traditional education create the kinds of divergent, independent thinkers that are really successful in today's increasingly automated and outsourced economy? As long as school effectiveness is determined by a one-right-answer mentality, schools will, at best, give lip service to creativity. But when individual teachers and schools become innovative themselves, the likelihood of graduates practicing creative thinking increases as well.

Becoming Personally More Creative—Every Day

I've saved writing about personal creativity until last because I, like many others, am uncertain about my own ability to innovate. I may never write a symphony or a novel. It's unlikely you will see something I've created hanging in the Louvre. Don't look for my name when announcing entrepreneur of the year awards. If I have any creative abilities, they fall firmly in the little-c category—finding new ways to solve everyday problems.

And that is not all bad.

Now and then, I do have a little spark of inspiration that helps me do my job a little better, helps me understand my world somewhat better, and perhaps helps others when I share my ideas through my writing.

I consciously do a few things that I feel increase my odds of gaining new insights. I walk each day over my lunch hour *without* earbuds. Apparently, I am not the only person who gets inspiration and new ideas while walking. A study by Stanford University shows that one is 60 percent more creative when walking—either indoors or outdoors (Briggs, 2014). I do my creative work in the morning. Morning, afternoon, or the wee small hours—it makes no difference, but learn your most mentally active time and use it. To the extent you can schedule your days, use your low times for meetings, reading, or napping.

I explore outside the lines, reading very few books on educational technology, although that is my primary job responsibility. Instead, I read about how technology is being used in other walks of life and ask what education can learn. Courtney O'Connell (2014) writes, "When faced with a problem, [innovative educators] don't just look at what another teacher does or how another school solved the problem. Disruptive educators look to *Fast Company* or the latest blog post from Seth Godin [sethgodin.typepad.com] to forage for solutions." Read broadly. Read weirdly. Read outside the lines. And then try to connect what you've learned to your work and life.

Playing the devil's advocate whenever I get the chance is one of my favorite, but probably most annoying, characteristics. One of Jeffrey Dyer, Hal Gregersen, and Clayton Christensen's "Five Skills of Disruptive Innovators" is *Questioning*. "Innovators ask a ton of questions. In fact, they treat the world as a question. . . . Innovators ask 'why.' They are the kid at the back of the class the teacher hates (and often, the person in the meeting the manager hates). Not only does this help you filter bullshit, but it helps jolt people from the status quo" (quoted in Parrish, 2013).

As I argued in Chapter 5, I am at my most creative when trying to solve a real—and important—problem. I personally find creativity for the sake of creativity rather boring. Seek out those tough nuts to crack, those insurmountable obstacles, those unreachable students or coworkers and use your imagination, your personal talents, and all your creative skills to do what to most others seems impossible.

In exploring creativity for this book, I was surprised to learn what an amorphous and highly personal attribute it actually is. Please define *creativity* in a way that has meaning to you. Please encourage creativity in your students in ways that make sense to you. Please find a perfect balance between craftsmanship and innovation when you assess student work.

But please, honor creativity and the students who demonstrate it. It's too important to both their futures and society's future for any teacher to dismiss it.

Teach outside the lines.

Up for Discussion

1. Do our communities want schools to produce conformists and rule followers or nonconformists and divergent thinkers? Or do parents, businesses, and higher ed not know what they want?

2. Can you answer Spencer's question, "How do we create structures and policies that encourage students to work creatively even when things get tough, boring or confusing?"

3. What evidence do you have that your own school's climate either fosters or discourages innovative thinking?

4. How important is it for a teacher to demonstrate creativity professionally? How can you improve the odds of you personally being innovative?

References

Adobe Systems. (2012, November 7). *Creativity and education: Why it matters.* Retrieved from http://www.adobe.com/aboutadobe/pressroom/pdfs/Adobe_Creativity_and_Education_Why_It_Matters_study.pdf

American Association of School Librarians. (2007). *Standards for the 2st-century learner.* Retrieved from http://www.ala.org/aasl/standards-guidelines/learning-standards

Anderson, L. W., & Krathwohl, D. R. (2001). *A taxonomy for learning, teaching and assessing: A revision of Bloom's taxonomy of educational objectives.* New York, NY: Longman.

Apple Inc. (2014). *iPad in education.* Retrieved from http://www.apple.com/education/ipad/apps-books-and-more

Aufderheide, P., & Jaszi, P. (2008). *Recut, reframe, recycle: Quoting copyrighted material in user-generated video.* Center for Social Media. Retrieved from http://www.cmsimpact.org/sites/default/files/CSM_Recut_Reframe_Recycle_report.pdf

Autor, D., & Price, B. (2013). *The changing task composition of the US labor market: An update of Autor, Levy, and Murnane.* Retrieved from http://economics.mit.edu/files/9758

Breen, B. (2004, December). The 6 myths of creativity. *Fast Company.* Retrieved from http://www.fastcompany.com/51559/6-myths-creativity

Briggs, S. (2014, May 3). We're about to tell you the secret to creativity, and you may NOT want to sit down. *informED.* Retrieved from http://www.opencolleges.edu.au/informed/news/creativity-and-walking/

Bronson, P., & Merryman, A. (2010, July 10). The creativity crisis. *Newsweek.* Retrieved from http://www.newsweek.com/creativity-crisis-74665

Brookhart, S. M. (2013, February). Assessing creativity. *Educational Leadership, 70*(5), 28–34. Retrieved from http://www.ascd.org/publications/educational-leadership/feb13/vol70/num05/Assessing-Creativity.aspx

Brooks, D. (2014, March 31). The employer's creed. *New York Times.* Retrieved from http://www.nytimes.com/2014/04/01/opinion/brooks-the-employers-creed.html?_r=0

Buck Institute for Education. (2014). *Why project based learning (PBL)?* Retrieved from http://bie.org/about/why_pbl

Clifford, M. (2012, November 26). *30 things you can do to promote creativity*. Retrieved from http://www.opencolleges.edu.au/informed/features/30-things -you-can-do-to-promote-creativity-in-your-classroom/#ixzz3J4LC99f8

Cohen, M. (2006). *First grade takes a test*. New York, NY: Star Bright Books.

Csikszentmihalyi, M. (1997). *Creativity: Flow and the psychology of discovery and invention*. New York, NY: Harper.

Dodge, J. (2009). *25 quick formative assessments for a differentiated classroom*. New York, NY: Scholastic.

Duckworth, A. L. (2003, April). *The key to success* [Video file]. Retrieved from https://www.ted.com/talks/angela_lee_duckworth_the_key_to_success_grit

Dweck, C. S. (2006). *Mindset: The new psychology of success*. New York, NY: Random House.

Falcone, D. (2013, June 1). *Noam Chomsky on democracy and education in the 21st century and beyond*. Truthout. Retrieved from http://www.truth-out.org/opinion/ item/16651-noam-chomsky-on-democracy-and-education-in-the-21st-century -and-beyond

Ferro, S. (2014, February 24). Study: Cheating fuels creativity. *Fast Company*. Retrieved from http://www.fastcodesign.com/3026764/asides/study-cheating -fuels-creativity

Florida, Richard. (2003). *The rise of the creative class*. New York, NY: Basic Books.

Gardner, H. (1993). *Frames of mind: The theory of multiple intelligences*. New York, NY: Basic Books.

Google. (2014). *Google Science Fair 2014*. Retrieved from https://www .googlesciencefair.com/en/

Heick, T. (2013, February 12). 10 ways to fake a 21st century classroom. *Te@ch Thought*. Retrieved from http://www.teachthought.com/teaching/10-ways-to -fake-a-21st-century-classroom

HuffPost Healthy Living. (2013, September 24). *Everything you thought you knew about creativity is wrong*. Retrieved from http://www.huffingtonpost .com/2013/09/23/creativity-myths_n_3963085.html

IBM. (2010, May 18). *IBM 2010 Global CEO Study: Creativity selected as most crucial factor for future success*. Retrieved from http://www-03.ibm.com/press/us/en/ pressrelease/31670.wss

International Baccalaureate Programme. (2014). *Diploma Programme curriculum— Core requirements*. Retrieved from http://www.ibo.org/en/programmes/diploma- programme/curriculum/

International Olympic Committee. (2014). *Dick Fosbury—High jump men— Athletics* [Video file]. Retrieved from http://www.olympic.org/videos/dick -fosbury-high-jump-men-athletics

International Society for Technology in Education. (2007). *ISTE standards for students*. Retrieved from http://www.iste.org/docs/pdfs/20-14_ISTE_Standards-S_PDF.pdf

Johnson, D. (2009, January/February). Building the capacity for empathy. *Library Media Connection, 31*(4), 98.

Kelley, T., & Kelley, D. (2012, December). Reclaim your creative confidence. *Harvard Business Review*. Retrieved from https://hbr.org/2012/12/reclaim-your -creative-confidence

Koehler, M. J. (2011). *What is TPACK?* Retrieved from http://www.matt-koehler .com/tpack/what-is-tpack/

Kohn, A. (1999). *Punished by rewards: The trouble with gold stars, incentive plans, A's, praise, and other bribes*. New York, NY: Houghton Mifflin.

Kozol, J. (1992). *Savage inequalities: Children in America's schools*. New York, NY: Harper.

Kraemer, K. L., Linden, G., & Dedrick, J. (2011). *Capturing value in global networks: Apple's iPad and iPhone*. Retrieved from http://www.readbag.com/pcic-merage-uci -papers-2011-value-ipad-iphone

Krugman, P. (2012, June 13). Sympathy for the Luddites. *New York Times*. Retrieved from http://www.nytimes.com/2013/06/14/opinion/krugman -sympathy-for-the-luddites.html

Larmer, J. (2014, February 6). *How can we teach and assess creativity and innovation in PBL?* [Web log post]. Buck Institute for Education. Retrieved from http://bie.org/blog/how_can_we_teach_and_assess_creativity_and_innovation_ in_pbl

Levy, F., & Murnane, R. (2004, October). Education and the changing job market. *Educational Leadership, 62*(2), 80–83.

MacLeod, H. (2009). *Ignore everybody: And 39 other keys to creativity*. New York, NY: Portfolio.

Macrorie, K. (1988). *The I-Search paper: Revised edition of searching writing*. Portsmouth, NH: Heinemann.

Maker Media. (2014). *MakerSpace: A new online community from Make*. Retrieved from http://makerspace.com/

McCusker, S. (2013, April 21). *5 ways to blow the top off of rubrics* [Web log post]. Retrieved from http://www.freetech4teachers.com/2013/04/5-ways-to-blow-top -off-of-rubrics.html#.VGdnIfnF9Ik

Michalko, M. (2011, December 6). *Twelve things you were not taught in school about creative thinking*. The Creativity Post. Retrieved from http://www.creativitypost .com/create/twelve_things_you_were_not_taught_in_school_about_creative_ thinking

Morelock, M. J., & Feldman, D. H. (1999). Prodigies. In M. Runco & S. Pritzker (Eds.), *Encyclopedia of creativity* (pp. 1303–1310). San Diego, CA: Academic Press.

Moulton, J. (2009, August 21). *It's time to get serious about creativity in the classroom*. Edutopia. Retrieved from http://www.edutopia.org/freedom-structure -balance-classroom

New York Times Editorial Board. (2013, December 7). Who says math has to be boring? *New York Times.* Retrieved from http://www.nytimes.com/2013/12/08/opinion/sunday/who-says-math-has-to-be-boring.html?_r=1&

Nicol, D., & MacFarlane-Dick, D. (2006). Formative assessment and self-regulated learning: A model and seven principles of good practice. *Studies in Higher Education, 31*(2), 199–218.

Nudell, Ric. (2013, February 21*). Evidence of creative problem solving rubric* [Web log post]. Retrieved from http://doug-johnson.squarespace.com/blue-skunk-blog/2013/2/21/a-creativity-rubric-by-ric-nudell.html

O'Connell, C. (2014, January 27). *5 habits of innovative educators.* HuffPost. Retrieved from http://www.huffingtonpost.com/courtney-oconnell/5-habits-of-highly-innovative-educators_b_4639434.html

Olien, J. (2013, December). *Inside the box: People don't actually like creativity.* Retrieved from http://www.slate.com/articles/health_and_science/science/2013/12/creativity_is_rejected_teachers_and_bosses_don_t_value_out_of_the_box_thinking.html

Organisation for Economic Co-operation and Development. (2014). *Measuring innovation in education: A new perspective.* Paris, France: Author. Retrieved from http://www.oecd-ilibrary.org/education/measuring-innovation-in-education_9789264215696-en

Papert, S. (1993). *Mindstorms: Children, computers, and powerful ideas* (2nd ed.). New York, NY: Basic Books.

Parrish, S. (2013, December 9). *The five skills of disruptive innovators* [Web log post]. Retrieved from http://www.farnamstreetblog.com/2013/12/the-five-skills-of-disruptive-innovators/

Partnership for 21st Century Learning. (2011). *P21 Framework Definitions document.* Retrieved from http://www.p21.org/storage/documents/P21_Framework_Definitions.pdf

Pink, D. H. (2006). *A whole new mind: Why right right-brainers will rule the future.* New York, NY: Riverhead.

Robinson, K. (2006, February). *How schools kill creativity* [Video file]. Retrieved from http://www.ted.com/talks/ken_robinson_says_schools_kill_creativity

Robinson, K. (with Aronica, L.). (2009). *The element: How finding your passion changes everything.* New York, NY: Viking.

Segev, E. (2013, May 9). *When there is a correct answer: Exercise in creative thinking* [Video file]. Retrieved from https://www.youtube.com/watch?v=9TskeE43Q1M#t=107

Sparks, S. D. (2011, December 13). Studies explore how to nurture students' creativity. *Education Week.* Retrieved from http://www.edweek.org/ew/articles/2011/12/14/14creative.h31.html

Spencer, J. (2014, January 27). When creativity isn't fun [Web log post]. *edrethink.* Retrieved from http://www.educationrethink.com/2014/01/when-creativity-isnt-fun.html

Thomas, S., Joseph, C., Laccetti, J., Mason, B., Mills, S., Perril, S., & Pullinger, K. (2007, December). Transliteracy: Crossing divides. *First Monday, 12*(12). Retrieved from http://firstmonday.org/ojs/index.php/fm/article/view/2060/1908

Townsend, J. (2014, April 10). Why playful learning is key to prosperity. *Forbes.* Retrieved from http://www.forbes.com/sites/ashoka/2014/04/10/why-playful -learning-is-the-key-to-prosperity/

Treffinger, D. J., Young, G. C., Selby, E. C., Shepardson, C., & Center for Creative Learning. (2002). *Assessing creativity: A guide for educators.* Storrs, CT: National Research Center/GT. Retrieved from http://www.gifted.uconn.edu/nrcgt/reports/ rm02170/rm02170.pdf

Tucker, M. (2014, January 14). PISA denial: Another flavor. *Education Week.* Retrieved from http://blogs.edweek.org/edweek/top_performers/2014/01/pisa_ denial_another_flavor.html

Westby, E. L., & Dawson, V. L. (1995). Creativity: Asset or burden in the classroom. *Creativity Research Journal, 8*(1), 1–10.

Wiggins, G. (2013a). *How to create a rubric that does what you want it to.* Te@ch-Thought. Retrieved from http://www.teachthought.com/teaching/how-to-create -a-rubric-that-does-what-you-want-it-to/

Wiggins, G. (2013b). How *to use a rubric without stifling creativity*. Te@chThought. Retrieved from http://www.teachthought.com/teaching/how-to-use-a-rubric -without-stifling-creativity/

Williams, R. (2008). *The non-designers design book* (3rd ed.). Berkeley, CA: Peachpit Press.

Additional Resources

Berger, R. (2003). *An ethic of excellence: Building a culture of craftsmanship with students.* Portsmouth, NH: Heinemann.

Byrne, R. (2014, January 7). *Five apps that help students start creative stories* [Web log post]. Retrieved from http://ipadapps4school.com/2014/01/07/five-ipad-apps -that-help-students-start-creative-stories/

Chapin, T. (n.d.). *Not on the test* [Video file]. Retrieved from http://www .notonthetest.com/index.html

Churches, A. (n.d.). *Bloom's digital taxonomy.* Educational Origami. Retrieved from http://edorigami.wikispaces.com/Bloom%27s+Digital+Taxonomy

Churches, A. (2008, April 1). *Bloom's taxonomy blooms digitally.* Tech Learning. Retrieved from http://teachnology.pbworks.com/f/Bloom%5C%27s+Taxonomy+ Blooms+Digitally.pdf

Ciotti, G. (2013, March 15). Nine of the best ways to boost creative thinking [Web log post]. *Lifehacker.* Retrieved from http://lifehacker.com/5990617/nine-of -the-best-ways-to-boost-creative-thinking

Coffee, S. (2013, August 19). *Top ten myths about creativity.* ArtsHub. Retrieved from http://www.artshub.co.uk/news-article/features/all-arts/top-ten-myths -about-creativity-196291

Cramond, B. (2005). *Fostering creativity in gifted students.* Waco, TX: Prufrock Press.

Cropley, A. J. (2012). *Creativity in education and learning: A guide for teachers and educators.* New York, NY: Routledge.

Darrow, D. (2013, July 24). *Creativity on the run: 18 apps that support the creative process.* Edutopia. Retrieved from http://www.edutopia.org/blog/apps-for -creativity-diane-darrow

Ditkoff, M. (2008, April 7). *100 simple ways to be more creative on the job* [Web log post]. Retrieved from http://www.ideachampions.com/weblogs/archives/2008/04/ post_7.shtml

Duckworth, A. L., & Quinn, P. D. (2009). Development and validation of the short grit scale (Grit–S). *Journal of Personality Assessment, 91*(2), 166–174. Retrieved from http://www.tandfonline.com/doi/abs/10.1080/002238908026 34290#.VGuIEfnF9Ik

Farr, C. (2014, April 24). *No courses, no classrooms, no grades—Just learning.* Mindshift. Retrieved from http://blogs.kqed.org/mindshift/2014/04/no-courses -no-classrooms-no-grades-just-learning/

Holderman, E. (2014, February 21). 15 best tech creation tools [Web log post]. *Common Sense graphite.* Retrieved from https://www.graphite.org/blog/15-best -tech-creation-tools

Kleon, A. (2012). *Steal like an artist: 10 things nobody told you about being creative.* New York, NY: Workman.

Krueger, N. (2014, January 15). What if kids hold the solutions to our biggest problems? [Web log post]. *ISTE Connects.* Retrieved from http://blog.iste.org/kids -hold-solutions-biggest-problems/

Lehrer, J. (2012). *Imagine: How creativity works.* Boston, MA: Houghton Mifflin.

Martinez, S. L., & Stager G. S. (2013). *Invent to learn: Making, tinkering, and engineering in the classroom.* La Vergne, TN: Lightning Source.

Paul, A. M. (2012, May 4). *Are we writing the creativity out of kids?* Mindshift. Retrieved from http://blogs.kqed.org/mindshift/2012/05/are-we-wringing-the -creativity-out-of-kids/

Porter, J. (2014, February 12). Can creativity really be taught? *Fast Company.* Retrieved from http://www.fastcompany.com/3026327/leadership-now/can -creativity-really-be-taught

Robelen, E. W. (2012, February 2). States mulling creativity index. *Education Week.* Retrieved from http://www.edweek.org/ew/articles/2012/02/02/19 creativity_ep.h31.html

Stix, M. (2014, March 29). *Teen to government: Change your typeface, save millions.* CNN Living. Retrieved from http://www.cnn.com/2014/03/27/living/student -money-saving-typeface-garamond-schools/index.html

Valenza, J. (2011, September 11). Fifty ways to leave your term paper/book report & tell your story [Web log post]. *School Library Journal.* Retrieved from http://

blogs.slj.com/neverendingsearch/2011/09/11/fifty-ways-to-leave-your-term
-paper-or-book-report-and-tell-your-story/

Zhao, Y. (2012). *World class learners: Educating creative and entrepreneurial students.*
Thousand Oaks, CA: Corwin.

Websites for Computer Applications Organized by Bloom's Taxonomy

Educational Origami (Web log): https://edorigami.wikispaces.com/
Bloom's+Digital+Taxonomy (Churches)

Educational Technology and Mobile Learning: http://www.educatorstechnology
.com/2013/01/new-version-of-blooms-taxonomy-for-ipad.html

iLearn Technology (blog): http://ilearntechnology.com/?tag=blooms-taxonomy

Kathy Schock's Guide to Everything: http://www.schrockguide.net/bloomin-apps
.html

Web 2.0 Tools Based on Bloom's Digital Taxonomy: http://www.chambersburg
.k12.pa.us/education/components/scrapbook/default.php?sectionid=2365

Index

A SAGE Company